the Empowered PRINCIPAL

Advance Praise

The Empowered Principal is a sensational read that portrays Angela's compassion for our educators and children. Angela is a gentle hand reaching out to lock arms with you and walk you through the tools you need to lead your school with tenacity and empathy. Angela helps school leaders lighten their load and release their anxiety. This book will help educators manage their mind, make decisions from a calmer place, and free up space in their brain to tackle issues for the teachers and the children they support.

Christina Mars
Client of Angela Kelly Coaching

Finally! A book that addresses the emotional resiliency that it takes to be a leader in education! If we expect our students to learn to be emotionally resilient, shouldn't it start with us? This book addresses the unique topic of the stamina and resilience it takes to be an educator or school district leader. Any educator or school leader who is experiencing burnout will benefit from the practical, time-tested strategies for responding to your thoughts and emotions throughout the work day. Reading *The Empowered Principal* brought me a whole new awareness and hope that finding greater balance really is possible.

Sarah Schroeder
Elementary teacher and parent of two

The Empowered Principal is a priceless resource for educators at all levels. Angela's front line experiences as a school principal and district administrator combined with her powerful life coaching skills make her book a game-changer for school leaders everywhere.

Bonnie Holub
Client and former public-school administrator and community college director

Angela Kelly Robeck is empowering principals everywhere! In my work as an elementary school principal, she has shown me how to make decisions from a more empowered state using the STEAR cycle. She is affirming, thought-provoking, reflective, and timely! She shares her wealth of experiences with honesty and deep insights connected to research-based strategies that have moved me to a more emotionally fit state. She truly has given me the tools to help me be an empowered principal! Thank you, Angela, for doing the important work you are doing!

Shanti Gallegos
Principal, Dulles Elementary

Angela Kelly's book, *The Empowered Principal*, is a must read for any school leader. Whether you are new to leadership or are considering making a change after a long career, you will find Kelly's coaching and writing to be thoughtful, honest, and engaging. Her guidance through the STEAR method has helped me to see my path forward to a career that is fulfilling and balanced. Be prepared to grow, learn, and find your happiness!

Carla Smith

Principal, Horizon Middle School West

The Empowered Principal is full of valuable insight and guidance. For those feeling stuck in the decision-making process, Angela's experience and wisdom provides useful and practical ways to help make decisions from a place of integrity and confidence.

Angela Rozzoni,

Client

the Empowered PRINCIPAL

The School Leader's
Alternative to
Career Burnout

Angela Kelly
Robeck

NEW YORK

LONDON • NASHVILLE • MELBOURNE • VANCOUVER

the Empowered PRINCIPAL

The School Leader's Alternative to Career Burnout

Published in New York, New York, by Morgan James Publishing in partnership with Difference Press. Morgan James is a trademark of Morgan James, LLC.
www.MorganJamesPublishing.com

ISBN 9781642793888 paperback
ISBN 9781642793895 eBook
ISBN 9781642793901 audioBook
Library of Congress Control Number: 2018914254

Cover Design by:
Rachel Lopez
www.r2cdesign.com

Interior Design by:
Christopher Kirk
www.GFSstudio.com

Morgan James is a proud partner of Habitat for Humanity Peninsula and Greater Williamsburg. Partners in building since 2006.

Get involved today! Visit
MorganJamesPublishing.com/giving-back

Dedications

To Mom: This one's for you
To Dad: For knowing I was an author all along

Table of Contents

Foreword

There are people who talk about wanting change in major institutions around the world, and spend their time fighting what is, and there are people who go out and *be* the change they know is possible. You see their belief, because they live it every single day.

They don't wait for the world to change and be different, they don't wait to take control when things are easier or they have more time, they go out and they just start making the change. They do this, because that is who they are at their core. And they couldn't possibly be any other way. It's in their DNA. It's in their decisions every single day. They just see the world differently. They focus on what it could be, not what it is.

These people pave the way for others to step into the change they imagine as well. They pass along courage and grit. Compassion and grace.

They focus on possibility.

People like Martin Luther King Junior, Princess Diana, Steve Jobs, and Malala Yousafzai.

In her book, "I am Malala," Nobel Prize winning Yousafzai writes of the Pakistani education crisis, "If one man can destroy everything, why can't one girl change it."

The world, our country, our education system need more fighters for change.

And I am eternally proud that my friend, colleague, and client for over three years, is one of those people.

This book brought tears to my eyes. In every single page, I feel Angela's love and determination to make education what she sees it could be. She doesn't just share a vision. She shares tangible, applicable steps on how to completely change your experience as an educator step by step.

To have been there, to have watched her *do* all the things she shares in this meticulously crafted book, is to see integrity.

Every single page is carefully crafted to pack in years of experience, deep transformation, and teachable tools, that can be passed on to every single colleague you meet.

Angela *is* the change.

And you can be too.

I highly recommend to not skip a page. Keep this with you, in your work bag, every single day.

This is the key, the answer, to loving a career in education, or lovingly walking away from it.

I always tell my clients to make sure they have done all the work that Angela has carefully crafted in these pages, before they make their decisions to stay or go, because worse than the pain of walking away, is the pain of regret if it wasn't the right choice.

Angela will lead you where you need to go powerfully – as she has so many other clients.

And where you need to go, is totally up to you. The answer lies in these pages.

Stacey Smith
Owner of Stacey Smith Coaching and
Founder of Diva Business School

1

The Struggle Was Real

I bet you thought that being the boss was going to be amazing. I am guessing you believed that you would finally get to make the changes at your site you desperately craved as a classroom teacher. Perhaps you've been able to hold conversations about making improvements, yet the ideas never seem to get fully implemented. You had no idea the quantity of demands that are placed on a school leader. You find yourself scurrying from one meeting to the next, talking about the latest best practices with little faith that you'll ever have time to implement them. You are now coming to work each day wondering why the job even matters and dreaming of a life that involves late mornings, coffee, and yoga pants – anything but emails, evening meetings, and rainy-day recess.

What I've come to learn is that most school principals are in the same boat. They too are disillusioned by the reality of the job. There are hundreds, if not thousands of teachers like yourself, who took the leap into school administration thinking they would be able to handle challenges and solve

1

problems with ease. Yet when they get into the daily grind, they find themselves overwhelmed and frustrated just like the last school leader. What is going on? Why does this job seem to chew people up and spit them out? How do some leaders find their way while others are left in a cloud of confusion, complaints, and consternation?

Trust me, your efforts have not gone unnoticed. I know you have tried everything to keep up with your to-do list. You wake up early to get a head start on emails that came in between midnight and 5:00 a.m. and double check your calendar to ensure that you aren't late for your first meeting of the day. You delegate so much to your secretary that you sometimes wonder if she is in fact the boss of the school instead of you. You visit classrooms and take breaks with the kids at recess to remind yourself of why you wanted this job in the first place. You call your colleagues to check in and see how they're doing, only to feel like they have it all pulled together while you are swimming in a pool of hot mess.

On one hand, you want to want the job. You want to love being a principal. Everyone else seems to love that you're in charge. Parents of your students ask you how you manage do it and your own parents have bragging rights that their daughter is the big cheese at school. Your non-teacher friends think that teaching 25 five-year-olds was crazy enough, but dealing with 40 staff members, 500 students, and thousands of parents and community members is the definition of insanity. When you go to parties, people always respond with gratitude for the work you are doing

– probably because they know they could never do what you do.

Yet, even with all the accolades, you are not happy. You do not find joy in the work. You really want to, but you just don't. You dream of loving the job as much as you love the paycheck but, instead, you shove down the feelings of disappointment and depression and kick into robotic mode. What's left is an outer shell that resembles you filled with an emptiness you cannot put your finger on. You dream of changing careers altogether, then resign to the fact you have no idea what else you'll do. It's back to working for the weekend and taking whatever drama comes your way.

How did this happen? How did becoming a school leader turn you into a work zombie who pretends she thrives on the fast pace of leadership but secretly loathes every single workday? You know in your head that you are not this person you've become, but you have no idea how to change the way you are feeling and stop this cycle of insanity. If you are like me, I'm guessing you've spent end-less nights trying to solve the mystery by reading books, listening to podcasts, printing out inspirational quotes, and journaling to find an answer. You believe that if only you could find a way to love your job so that you can hold on to all you've worked so hard for, life would be so much better.

Yet, in the meantime, you are working from the time you wake up until you crash at night. You miss out on per-sonal events because you have school events at night and on the weekends. You find yourself staying in principal mode when you get home and barking orders at your husband and kids. While you sip on a gin and tonic, you dream of walking into the district office and resigning tomorrow but the angst of no paycheck brings you back to reality. You look into the mirror and see how you've aged over the last couple of years. You observe the wrinkles, weight gain, and a few grey hairs poking out from the part of your hair. You think to yourself "I look like I'm a former president! My job cannot be as stressful as that job!" Yet it feels that stressful. You're at a complete loss.

Let me offer you some hope. I have been in your shoes and I was at a loss just like you. Being a principal is no simple task. It requires stamina, patience, skill, and contemplation. It takes an incredible amount of effort, and I can relate to dreaming of the day that I would drop the keys off one last time and not let the door hit me in the bum. However, before you run off to Tahiti with nothing with a bathing suit and open a tiki bar, let's see if we can dive a little more into what your heart is authentically seeking.

Since you are reading this book, I'm under the impression that you feel trapped between wanting to maintain your position in education and wanting to quit this job and find a career in something less stressful. Let me guess. You'd leave if you could but the money is too good, the benefits are nice, and your pension will be killer if you can just stand to work for 20 more years. You've worked so hard to earn this title and status, you have strong connections with your colleagues, and you have no idea what else you would do with the rest of your life if you weren't in education. Even if you did know what else you'd like to do, wouldn't your colleagues be in shock at your exit? Wouldn't family and friends tell you that you're crazy for leaving such a good job? Wouldn't you regret your decision to resign when your savings account bottomed out?

These fears feel so real. They seem like factual outcomes of your decision to quit the job. They feel so real that every time you contemplate leaving, you talk yourself out of it. In that case, let's take a look at your life from the angle of staying in the job. You decide that although you aren't happy and the job is not what you thought it would be, you can't leave because you need the money and you cannot imagine life without your current circles of connections. You don't have time to decide what else to do with all of your remaining time on earth, therefore working for another person is the simplest option. Even though the thought of two more decades of being a principal makes you physically ill, you figure you can sugar coat your way through it, repeating positive quotes and mantras to get you through to retirement, where you will finally be able to relax and have some fun.

Feeling even more uncertain about what to do?

Let me ask you this. What would it feel like to make the decision of staying or going from a place of knowing how to love either choice? Does this feel possible? I know. It seems like there is no way you can enjoy a job that kicks the ever-living daylight out of you day after day. Is it possible that after reading this book you could decide that you love the position and stay for years to come? Could you also be at peace with your tenure as principal and choose to try new endeavors?

What I have learned through my years of experience as a school leader along with my years of exposure to thought management and life coaching is this: You have the ability to love it and leave it at any time. You can choose to enjoy your position as a school leader. You can choose to be miserable as a school leader. You can choose to love the position while you are in it and resign to pursue other positions, careers, or interests. Glenda the Good Witch of the North was right. You've always had the power. You just have to learn it for yourself and I am going to show you how.

2

My Story

At the beginning of my tenure, I had very little confidence in my competency as a leader. I had no formal training on how to lead a team of 40 adults. I was inexperienced at budgets and meeting facilitation. I knew how to implement my classroom vision but managing a vision for an entire school seemed daunting. I spent a great deal of time passively thinking, planning, and preparing versus actively engaging in activities that were new to me. I can remember how long I would prepare myself for a school site council meeting. I agonized over the agenda items and how to present them. I feared I did not have enough knowledge on the topic so I would read and rehearse what I was going to say, and even then I led the meetings from a place of trepidation.

It took me a few years into the job to realize that the only way to really know how to do the job is to take action and do it! No amount of reading, studying, planning, preparing, thinking, or talking about running a powerful meeting will actually make you a powerful meeting facilitator.

The act of leading a meeting is what transforms you into a strong leader. Regardless of the outcome of the meeting, choosing to step into your position as a school leader by actively putting yourself out there is how you gain confidence. This holds true in every aspect of the job.

I've been in education my entire life – about half as a student and the other half as an educator. As a student I learned all of the socially acceptable skills that go along with being in school, such as standing in line, taking turns, and raising my hand before I speak (that one was really hard for me). I also learned lessons that were not in the curriculum, things like: tell the truth only when it's pleasant, good students are the only ones who get praised, and only the teacher makes decisions. I took these lessons to heart and worked to be the best little student I could be. I said the right answers, was sure to please the teacher, and never got sent to the principal's office. I did not ask questions that would offend or upset others and even when I wanted to speak up as I knew it was survival of the nicest. If you wanted to stay in the game and advance your ranking, you had to do whatever the adult in the room said. This method worked well for me through my formative years and into college. I was a strong, obedient student who followed the rules and got the A. It never occurred to me that my skill set honed as a student would not serve me well as an adult.

Who's the Boss?

Fast forward to 2010. I'd completed all the requirements necessary and secured my first position as an elementary school principal. I was hired as the principal of a brand-new school within my school district. Being a new principal of a new school was truly the blind leading the blind. While I was honored that my boss believed I was capable of this incredible feat, I was not sure how to be a principal, let alone how to create an entire series of new systems for a new school site. I felt overwhelmed, disillusioned, and deflated. I could not keep up with all I was expected to do. I questioned how I got myself into this situation. I was absolutely miserable, yet years of conditioning led me to believe that I should keep quiet and do the job I was hired to do. I approached the new position in the same way I'd approached being a student. However this time it was not working. I wasn't getting gold stars from the teacher. I wasn't being complimented on my penmanship or my extra credit completion. I was being pummeled with complaints, concerns, and criticism.

Nothing prepared me for the barrage of negativity I experienced as a principal. My game plan no longer worked. As a teacher, I led with velvet gloves and had the emotional resiliency of a toddler. I gained positive traction by showing up as a sweet, loving, and gentle kindergarten teacher. When I continued using this approach as a principal, I was faced with scrutiny and disapproval. People didn't want a soft and sappy leader. They wanted someone who was willing to make strong decisions and stand by those decisions. They were looking for certainty and competency, but most of all courage. I wanted to deliver on their demands and read all the leadership strategy books I could get my hands on. The tips were help-ful in how to execute the work, but there were no words of advice on how to manage the emotional sabotage of school leaders. I had little practice in dealing with antag-onistic feedback.

Fortunately into my second year, I stumbled across *Finding Your Own North Star* by Martha Beck. I imme-diately bought her book and was so intrigued by her work that I subsequently completed her life coach training pro-gram. It became so clear to me why I had been struggling. I was approaching my job in a constant state of fear. I was afraid of being disliked by my staff and the parent com-munity. I was worried I was not making the best instruc-tional choices for the students. I believed I was not capable of being decisive and bold. I based my approach to my job on a set of standards I'd set for myself way back in childhood. It had never occurred to me to consider why I placed so much emphasis on being liked and why I was so afraid of other people's disapproval. I gained insight on why some people sparked apprehension and negativity in me and how I could adjust the way I responded to them. As I strengthened the habit of managing my thoughts, I began to plan my day from a place of abundance instead of scarcity. I started to see that when I chose to believe I was capable of handling any situation that arose during the day, no matter what, that life as a principal became so much more tolerable.

I also recognized that strategies for building school leaders' emotional fitness and resiliency were non-existent.

We participated in trainings that recognized the need for emotional resilience – however, the focus was primarily on student mental and emotional well-being. Conversations involving emotional support for school leaders were swept under the rug. After all, we were already in a leadership position. It was assumed that we were capable of handling our emotions. When principals expressed emotional distress during district leadership team meetings, it was said that as leaders we should be able to problem solve on our own. There was no time built into our workweek for tending to our emotional needs as humans. We were too busy being busy.

Still, something told me that neglecting our emotions as educators was a significant contributor to the industry's high levels of attrition and low percentages of student achievement. I became a certified life coach through The Life Coach School under Brooke Castillo in 2015 and began sharing a variety of mind management tools with students, teachers, and parents. One was the STEAR cycle, which I will explain in detail later. Parents were so impressed with the STEAR cycle that they scheduled one on one appointments with me to dive deeper into understanding its process and how they might use it with their children at home. Teachers found it helpful when supporting students through social conflicts and gleaned some insight into their own emotional reactions to work and personal situations. I enjoyed being able to support my constituents and see how STEAR helped them supervise their thoughts and emotions.

While I enjoyed interjecting thought management tools into my work whenever possible, I continued to feel misaligned. I hired a personal coach and heavily relied on the STEAR cycle to manage my thoughts about the job, yet I yearned for a lifestyle that was more flexible and free of the school year demands and rigor. My heart ached to spend my days teaching others the power of the STEAR cycle. I just knew that if they could see how their thoughts impact their emotions and results, they too could start shifting to more intentional thoughts that better serve them. On the flip side, I continued to hold firmly to the belief that I relied on this job for steady income, benefits, and professional status. My mind was generating conflicting thoughts all day long.

I allowed my brain to argue with itself until my mom was diagnosed with an incurable medical condition. She was no longer able to travel and eventually became homebound. In order to spend time with her, I had to travel from my home in California to my home state of Iowa. As you can imagine, the school year schedule was not forgiving. I was struggling to meet the needs of my mom and the demands of the district. I shifted to a district level administrator position for one year, thinking that I could juggle both, but I found myself not being able to be with her when she most needed me. I attempted to take a leave of absence, and when that fell through, it became apparent to me that this was my time to boldly move forward with my life and rely on the magic of coaching and the universe to support me through the transition.

Making the Move

Deciding to leave my career in education after 25 years was one of the most challenging decisions I have made in my life. It required high level coaching and constant thought management. It insisted that I experience emotions I did not think I could endure. I had to lay my former identity to rest and give birth to a new me.

My decision to leave the profession and start a movement in bringing emotional fitness to education is both altruistic and personal. In all my years as a teacher, instructional coach, and school leader, I witnessed extensive amounts of suffering. Suffering occurs when the reality of your life conditions do not match your expectations. When life does not align with your expectations, you are unhappy. You suffer when you do not believe you have the power to change the misalignment. This happened on a daily basis in my school. Parents had expectations that were not met. Teachers wanted the curriculum and bell schedules to be different than they were. Students wanted longer recess and lunch breaks. Neighbors of the school wanted the school bells to ring softer and less often. The school board and district officials wanted site scores to be higher. Principals wanted people to stop interrupting them. There was so much suffering based on misaligned expectations and realities.

When I learned that suffering is optional, and I mean truly optional, I began wondering why we didn't learn thought management as children. Then I wondered, why aren't we learning it as adults? Why are there no courses in college on emotional fitness? There are plenty of courses on academia, the arts, and physical fitness, but very few if any, on mental and emotional health. It was this realization, along with my innate passion for personal development, that led me to my new mission of bringing emotional tools to the very people who have the greatest impact on our youth – educators. We must become models for our students. We must learn to lead schools with emotional resiliency and stamina. We need to see for ourselves and for our students that it is our thinking that determines the results we get in our lives.

Client Case: Claire

Take the example of one of my clients. Claire is a 42-year-old teacher, wife, and mother of two. After 15 years of teaching grade levels spanning from kindergarten to fifth grade, she chose to leave the classroom to become an instructional coach. Claire enjoyed supporting teachers in setting up their classrooms, defining classroom management routines, and planning lessons. She quickly learned, however, that not all teachers had her innate gift for teaching and was shocked at the spectrum of instructional strategies, management styles, and intense disgruntlement of some individuals. Claire found herself taking on the emotions of her fellow teachers and did not like the way she found herself feeling about her job.

Through personalized coaching, Claire was able to learn that she could work with people who were experiencing negative emotion without taking it upon herself. She became aware that her thoughts about their teaching practices directly influenced how she interacted with them. Over time, she was able to guide her thinking about other people and turn her thoughts into more productive ones. She regained her joy for teaching and learning and is currently working toward her administrative credential.

If you are still with me, I am absolutely convinced that you are my people. You see the need to adjust the way we approach teaching, learning, and school leadership. You're aching to feel more balance and want to be the model that your students and teachers so desperately need. You are ready to step into your personal power and make decisions about your career from a state of confidence and courage. Join me in learning how to change the way school leaders experience education, one thought at a time.

Deciding to take responsibility for your mental and emotional well-being is not for the faint of heart. I have the utmost of faith that you are up to the task. I will believe in you and hold space for you when you do not feel you are able to believe in yourself. I am here for you, every step of the way. Together, we will learn how to take back your ability to make intentional decisions for yourself and use your emotional stamina to embrace the work you do in the world. Whether it is continuing in education or shifting into something else, you'll be able to make all of your decisions from a place of personal empowerment.

3

The Solution Journey

B y now, you may be wondering how you can determine your own best next step. From my own experience and through working with my clients, I've discovered that the journey toward a fulfilling career goes through three stages.

Stage 1: Seeking Solutions

My journey to understand the source of my angst began out of desperation. Although I had support from the district team and a few of my teachers, I felt alone. I sought out any and every book available on school leadership, yet none of them had the solution I needed. I needed to feel better. I needed to have confidence and influence. I wanted to be the principal who, when she walked into a room, exuded enthusiasm, grace, and excellence. I wanted to be good at the job and feel good about the job, right now.

During my second year as principal, I signed up for Martha Beck's life coach training. I had little idea what life coaching was, but I was desperate to find solutions and be happy in my career. What I learned from her program was that I had been ignoring my soul's voice and desires by only allowing social expectations to drive my life's course. I made decisions with my head and not my heart and I rarely allowed myself to feel emotion – positive or negative. This insight sent me on a two-year pilgrimage of learning to lead my school and my life more from my heart and less from my head. This was a challenge for me because as a child I learned to navigate the world based on reason and rationale. I found it easier to negate and avoid any negative emotion versus using my emotions as a tool and a guide for leading my school and my life.

I experienced incredible resistance and vulnerability during this time as a leader. I did not want to take the time to process painful feelings. I contested my personal coach's nudges to let the school community see the real Angela. Yet, layer by layer, I began to peel back the shield I'd been living behind for so long and exposed myself to the harshness that comes with being a true leader. These were not my favorite years, but they were the most transformative for my internal world.

Stage 2: Setting the Stage

At the beginning of my third year, I transitioned back to the elementary school where I started my teaching career in California. I taught at this school for 15 years and it felt like I had come home. The staff and community graciously welcomed me and things were humming. My predecessor left things in great shape and I was finally starting to feel like I knew what I was doing most of the time. But as we know, it is when things feel comfortable that discomfort most often wants to visit.

Due to a variety of circumstances, our superintendent resigned mid-year. His departure left me feeling uncertain because I felt safe and protected by him. Even in my worst moments as a principal, he supported and guided me. His exit left me feeling lost once again. I dove back into personal development and researched many potential resources. This led me to The Life Coach School, which was founded by the fabulously smart and savvy Brooke Castillo. Brooke developed a comprehensive and rigorous coach training institution that offered a six-day full-immersion program with the option to become certified under The Life Coach School. I dropped into my heart once again and felt compelled to attend this program. I wasn't exactly sure why or how I was going to pull this off, but I knew with my soul that I needed to be there. What I gained from Brooke's program were tangible cognitive tools that made sense to my brain. Her work was the next set of strategies I needed to up level my game as a school leader. I learned how to manage my emotions in a way that more deeply impacted how I showed up at work. I spent the next year experimenting with various strategies to see how they might translate in the world of public education. I planned my year with my results first in mind. I decided ahead of time how I wanted parent meetings to go and matched my approach with my intended outcomes. I viewed critical feedback as a reflection of the person providing it versus making it mean I sucked at my job. It was a time of great relief and renewed enthusiasm.

Stage 3: Expedited Transformation

I began to feel an excitement for work that I'd never experienced. I was using the tools to manage my thinking and emotions in everything from parent meetings to district objectives. I treated others with so much more compassion and respect because I understood why they were acting the way they were and I understood why I acted the way I did. I felt more in control than I had ever felt before as a principal. I was confident in my ability to handle the job and I felt competent in the way I handled most issues. It felt on some level as if I had "arrived." Even though I felt better, the urge to change paths tugged at me. Whenever I looked at the career advancement opportunities ahead of me, nothing appealed to me. I had no desire to become a director or superintendent. Yet, the argument in my head was that I'd worked so hard to learn how to enjoy my job, why would I consider leaving it when there were so many reasons to stay?

It was then I decided I needed to end my mind's debate once and for all. Fortunately, I'd just attended The Life Coach School's annual mastermind weekend and reconnected with friends I'd met in my cohort. One woman in particular reached out to me and we spent much of our time at mastermind together. I shared with her the chatter in my head regarding my current leadership position and she shared with me that she was going all in on building her coaching business. I listened with admiration for her courage and commitment to starting such an endeavor. At the end of mastermind, we exchanged numbers and went back to our respective homes.

A few weeks later, Stacey called me to check in and asked if I'd like to coach with her on my struggle with my job. It seemed like fate. I quickly agreed and we got to work. To be honest, at the time I wasn't sure whether coaching would really help me figure this out. I mean, I'd been through two coaching certifications and I was still working on figuring out my life! But, I felt a deep sense of connection to Stacey and based on the risks she was taking in her business, I felt it would not hurt me to have some help with finding solutions.

What ensued over the next two years was deep self-reflection work and busting through mental blocks I never knew existed in my mind. Stacey's coaching approach made me feel so trusting and safe that it allowed me to open up and heal profound emotional wounds from my past. Cleaning up my thoughts about who I was as a person and how I was limiting my potential was not what I was expecting out of our coaching relationship, but it was the answer to everything. Stacey cultivated massive internal transformation within me so that I could produce massive external transformation in my external life. The rest of my story is history in the making!

From Fear to STEAR

What made the most difference for me was applying the STEAR cycle – one of the best strategies I've learned in self-coaching. The concept behind this tool has been discussed by numerous philosophers, academicians, scholars, and coaches for thousands of centuries, and still holds true today. While its premise is straightforward, its application can be challenging to the brain. The beauty of this powerful tool is that it provides a concrete way of looking at situations at work or in your personal life and allows you to observe your brain in motion.

The STEAR Cycle

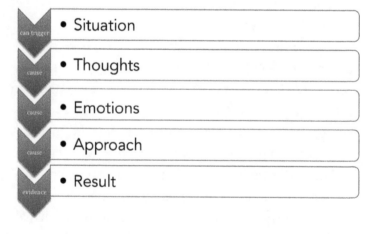

The STEAR cycle was developed under the premise that our thoughts create our emotions, our emotional state impacts our approach to life situations, and the way we choose to approach situations provides us with a result. Seem too simple to be true? I'll start by saying I did not learn this practice overnight. It's taken time and support from my coaches to get from where you are today to where I am today. The good news is this – I was able to figure out how to live a more empowered life by applying the STEAR cycle over time and I can expedite your empowerment by showing you the way.

As I shared briefly in the first chapter, the STEAR cycle is a tool you can use to observe the way your brain is thinking. This is critical in every way because human thoughts create human emotions. Once you see this in action, you will begin to understand yourself and other people's behavior in an entirely new light. It is from this awareness that you will be able to take charge of your life and STEAR it in the direction you want.

- **S = Situation:** A situation is anything outside of your control. It is completely neutral. It can be a person, place, thing, event, or circumstance.
- **T = Thought:** A thought is a sentence that occurs in your mind.
- **E = Emotion:** An emotion is how you are feeling, described in a word or set of words.
- **A = Approach:** Your approach is the action or set of actions you choose to take based on your emotional state. It is what you do or do not do.
- **R = Result:** A result is what occurs from your reaction, inaction, or taking action.

The STEAR cycle is always at play. It is constantly running whether we are aware of it or not. Let's take a common situation at school and see how the STEAR cycle looks when it is in motion.

It's the last week before all teacher observations must be completed. You have one teacher who has rescheduled her observation for the third time. She's been resistant to all of her observation appointments and has rescheduled her prior observations at least once. You are convinced she is avoiding her observations in an attempt to push past the contractual deadline. She knows that if you don't get into her room before the deadline, that you are not able to conduct any further formal observations. This makes you furious because you have concerns about her classroom management and want to document them using a formal format. You decide that you aren't going to take this from her anymore and you march to her room to tell her that you will not reschedule the observation again. When you talk with her, your blood is boiling and you are trying to keep your face from snarling and your volume down. Sensing your frustration, she lashes back at you saying that it's not her fault. The music teacher had to reschedule the music class lesson, and she scheduled it at the same time as the observation. You snap back and tell the teacher to cancel the music lesson so you can keep the scheduled observation time. She mutters under her breath as you walk out. The next day, you overhear her telling her team what a witch you are and that you didn't even try to work with her on rescheduling.

If we analyze this situation using the STEAR cycle, here's what we would see:

Situation = Teacher observation

Thought = She's avoiding being observed.

Emotions = Angry, fuming, irritated

Approach = Dig in your heels, speak to her in anger, use positional power, and fail to listen and work with teacher.

Result = You get your way. She complains about you to colleagues. The music teacher is offended that she wasn't a part of the conversation. The kids miss out on music.

The thought that she was avoiding being observed triggered an intense emotional reaction. Being in an angry emotional state led you to march to her classroom and tear into her. Tearing into her led to you getting the result you thought you wanted, but with some additional results that you may not have wanted.

This is where the STEAR cycle gets interesting. You can play around with different thoughts to see how they might play out and provide you with different results. Let's go back to the exact situation but substitute in a different thought. The cycle might look something like this:

Situation: Teacher observation

Thought: She must be really nervous about being observed.

Emotions: Compassion, concern, care

Approach: Walk to her classroom and check in with her. Ask her why she needs to reschedule and how can you make the observation experience less uncomfortable.

Result: She explains about the music class and admits that she's nervous because she knows her classroom management needs work, but she isn't sure how to change or improve it at this point in the school year. You tell her you are happy to help her with that and you ask her if she has signed up to work with the school's instructional coach for additional support.

The STEAR cycle is the tool that will help you in both your professional and your personal life. In the following chapters, we'll break down each component so you can study the relationships between them and practice identifying the thoughts that underlie pessimistic emotions. I'll also be sure to provide an abundance of work-related examples for you to see how to implement the model in various situations.

Your Dream Life

One simple request before we get started: I want you to imagine waking up every day with so much enthusiasm for your life that you bounce out of bed with boundless energy. Suppose everyday life feels the same as you feel while on vacation. You love your job and cannot wait to get your day started! To get you in the mood, complete the following sentences. Write down the first thought that comes to mind.

- If money weren't an issue, I'd spend my time…
- If I didn't care what anyone else thought about my life, I would…
- If I were absolutely sure that I was on the right path, I would…
- If my success was guaranteed, I'd try…
- If I had the freedom to be me, I would…
- If I could create my ideal career, I would…

Getting your brain to believe that being happy is possible will stimulate an emotional state that allows you to explore options you never before conceived. Let's do this!

4

The STEAR Cycle in Motion

I n this chapter, we are going to take a look at a common work situation from multiple angles and use the STEAR cycle to dissect the way our brains function and how they work against us if we do not keep a close watch on them. I'll also give you an opportunity to fill in your own situation to observe how your brain is reacting while you are at work.

Let's first take a closer look at the STEAR cycle components. I want you to become so familiar with these components that you eventually become skilled at visualizing the cycle in real time.

The STEAR Cycle Components
S = Situation

A situation is anything outside of you. All situations are completely neutral and all are outside your sphere of control. They, in and of themselves, hold no meaning, therefore they are not innately positive or negative. A situation can be a person, a place, a thing, an event, or a circumstance.

Examples of situations include: the weather, a car accident, other people, other people's behavior, money, the economy, the president, our kids, our bosses, teachers, curriculum, and test scores.

T = Thought

A thought is a sentence that occurs in your mind. Our brains continually produce thoughts whether we are aware of them or not, and in fact, we often do not actively notice the majority of our thoughts. When we aren't aware of our thoughts, we don't realize their impact on our lives. We aren't able to consider them and question them. Examples of thoughts include: "I hope it doesn't rain during the walk-a-thon." "I wonder how this IEP will go?" "I need to make more money." "Our president is an idiot." "My child should do his homework." "My boss is so supportive." "I wish staff meetings were more productive." "This curriculum is awful." "If we don't improve test scores, my job will be in danger."

You cannot stop thoughts from occurring, but you can learn to become aware of them and how they guide your life in particular directions.

E = Emotions

Emotions are experienced as a vibration in the body. This is why we refer to them as feelings; because they can be felt within the body. Humans created words that describe these feelings in our body in order to communicate our emotional experience. While there are thousands of words to pinpoint the nuances of our emotions, we generally express our emotional state through words like happy, sad, angry, or scared.

Emotions are triggered by our thoughts. You can have a slight reaction or an intense reaction based on the meaning you've attached to a particular thought. Emotions are separate from sensations within the body. Sensations are involuntary and come from the body to relay information to the brain such as hunger, pain, and reflexes. Emotions come from the mind and relay vibrations to the body.

A = Approach

Your approach is the action or set of actions you choose to take toward a situation. It is both what you decide to do or not do. You always choose an approach, even if the approach of choice is not to take action. Not taking action *is* a form of action. The three general ways that people approach situations are through reaction, inaction, or intentional action. Reaction is an emotional response to the situation. Inaction is purposefully choosing not to take action. Intentional action is when you make a plan and act accordingly. We'll discuss each of these more in depth in Chapter 5.

R = Result

A result is the effect brought about by your approach. It is what comes from your reaction, inaction, or intentional action. Results are always happening; we just do not often connect our results to our approach. Results are also situations in the sense that they are not fully in our control. We can influence our outcome through our thinking, emotions, and choosing an approach that we believe will help us achieve a certain result, but we do not have full control over how the results play out. I will show you how you can decide on a result you want then use the STEAR cycle to help you determine your approach. This will help expedite your ability to achieve any goal you desire.

STEAR in Motion

We are going to take a look at some common situations and see how the STEAR cycle components interrelate. I've used some of these examples in my podcast and my listeners are always grateful to see how the cycle works in various situations that they can relate to as a school leader.

Let's use the beloved staff meeting. In my district, we had weekly staff meetings after school on Wednesdays. I personally loved attending staff meetings as a teacher. For me, it was an opportunity to see colleagues I typically didn't see the rest of the week. Being a social butterfly, I naturally used this time to communicate and collaborate, just not always at the most appropriate times! This scenario will take a look at a common staff meeting occurrence.

Situation: Two teachers are talking during the staff meeting.

This is a neutral event. It is outside of your control and outside of you.

Thought: They are being disrespectful.

Your thought that the teachers are being disrespectful gives the situation meaning. You see them talking and you make it mean that they are being disrespectful to you.

Emotion: Irritated

The thought that the teachers are being disrespectful triggers you into a state of irritation. You feel irritation because you believe they should not be talking and the reality is that they are talking.

Approach: Stop your presentation and ask them to stop talking while you are presenting.

Because you are in an agitated state, you decide to approach the teachers by reacting to your emotions. You stop presenting and speak to them in an irritated manner.

Result: Room gets quiet. People shift in their seats. The talking teachers stop talking and look down for the remainder of the staff meeting.

Your approach resulted in getting the teachers to stop talking, which most likely was your goal. However, other results occurred based on your choice of approach. Remember, no matter what approach you choose, you don't have full control over the outcome. You may or may not be impacted by the additional results. This result is also a new situation. Depending on how you think about this result, you may have another thought arise that triggers a new emotion.

Now, let's take a look at the same situation with a different thought.

Situation: Two teachers are talking during the staff meeting.

Again, this is a neutral event. It is outside of your control and outside of you.

Thought: I wonder if there are questions?

Same situation but a different thought emerges.

Emotion: Curious

This thought triggered a different emotional response. In this case, the thought "I wonder if there are questions?" stirs up some curiosity.

Approach: You pause the presentation and ask if there are any questions.

Your feeling of curiousness drives you to approach the teachers from a state of curiosity.

Result: One of the talking teachers says yes, and asks a question. Three other people raise their hands. Conversation ensues.

Your approach in offering people to ask questions resulted in multiple people having questions that opened up a conversation. Depending on your thought about the presentation being paused by questions and conversation, you may feel the situation was never a problem and resulted in deeper understanding or you may feel that it took your presentation off track. What you decide to make it mean comes from the thoughts that arise in your head.

In this scenario, the different thought triggered a very different emotional state that led to a different result. The key is to notice that thoughts trigger emotions based on what we make that sentence in our head mean. For this principal, the thought "I wonder if there are questions" stimulates a less intense vibration than the thought "They are being disrespectful." The reason for the difference in intensity is because behind the thought is a belief system that has determined being disrespected is a bad thing. We'll expand on belief systems in the next chapter.

Let's run one more cycle on this situation to demonstrate how our thinking impacts not only our emotions and results, but in the way we view ourselves as leaders.

Situation: Two teachers are talking during the staff meeting.

Same situation.

Thought: I can't keep my teachers' attention.

This time, the thought that occurs is about the principal. Her brain made the talking teachers mean that something is wrong with her.

Emotion: Ashamed

The principal is under the impression that she should be able to control teacher behavior and when teachers are not behaving in a way that she believes is positive or acceptable, she takes it upon herself.

Approach: Plow through your presentation and let the staff out early

The principal's emotional state leaves her feeling like no one cares about what she is saying, therefore she responds by speeding through her presentation and getting out of the uncomfortable situation as soon as possible.

Result: Teachers don't engage during the presentation.

Her approach of speeding through the presentation because she does not believe she is a good presenter leaves her teachers with no way to engage with her. This builds evidence for her brain that the thought she chose to believe is true in that she cannot hold her teachers' attention.

As you can see through this imaginary circumstance, changing the thought in your head can change the results you experience. This is of course an example and the results may vary. I'm not suggesting you try to control the outcome of every situation. This is not about control. Remember, you cannot control situations outside of yourself. What I am suggesting is that you can decide if you want to believe the thought that occurs in your brain. As you gain more awareness of the thoughts that emerge, you'll be able to stop and ask yourself "Do I believe this thought is true? Do I want to believe it is true? If not, what would I prefer to think about this situation?" It is easier said than done, but practicing awareness of your thoughts is the first step.

Client Case: Beth

A client I'll name Beth has been a principal for three years. She has a very gentle demeanor and does not speak up often in her leadership team meetings. She tends to feel intimidated by the other principals who are more exuberant and outspoken. Although she does not often share her ideas, when she does muster up the courage to speak up, she feels as though nobody listens or takes her input seriously. In one of our sessions, we ran the STEAR cycle to see if we could find out what was happening. Here's what we unveiled:

S = Leadership Team Meetings

T = Nobody listens to me.

E = Insignificant

A = Doesn't speak up during meetings.

R = Her ideas are not heard.

She leaves frustrated, and the changes she wants to recommend are never implemented.

When Beth believes that nobody listens to her, she then doesn't see a need to speak up in the first place. She holds her ideas in her head and grows more frustrated that she is not able to make the changes she believes will benefit her students and staff. My questions to her were these: "What is it costing your students for you to continue believing the thought that nobody listens to you? What could happen for your students if you believed that what you had to say was not only valuable to your students, but to all the students across the district?" We sat in silence for a while. She finally said, "Wow. I'd never thought of it that way. I've been so wrapped up in my own feelings that I never considered the impact my self-pity was having on my students." We then created a more intentional STEAR cycle that started with a new thought:

S = Leadership Team Meetings

T = My students deserve my leadership ideas.

E = Committed

A = Speak up even when I'm scared. Fully participate. Not make other people's feedback mean I am not significant.

R = Implement changes for my students

Do you see how the shift in thinking changes the entire energy level of Beth's purpose in her job? She feels completely dedicated to her students, yet her own feelings of insecurity were preventing her from taking care of them. Now that she views them as her compelling reason to push through her fears, her entire energy and focus has shifted toward being an empowered leader.

Your Turn!

Are you ready? Below are open STEAR cycles just waiting for you to give them a whirl. It is normal to get stuck on one of the components. If you do, just skip it and move on to the next component. For example, clients who are new to the STEAR cycle are often unsure what they are thinking. They can usually identify their emotion. Just skip to the emotion and see if a thought pops up as you work through the cycle. Try this with a couple of situations at work that are bringing up stress.

The STEAR Cycle

S = Situation
T = Thought
E = Emotion
A = Approach
R = Result

S =

_____

T =

_____

E =

_____

A =

_____

R =

_____

The STEAR Cycle
S = Situation
T = Thought
E = Emotion
A = Approach
R = Result

S =
_____

T =
_____

E =
_____

A =
_____

R =
_____

The STEAR cycle is a powerful tool that allows you to observe your thought process so you can see the connection between thoughts, emotions, and actions and how these three impact the results in your life. With this tool, you will be able to make decisions from a place of empowerment and design a life that best suits your professional and personal goals.

Summary
- The STEAR cycle is always in motion.
- You can observe situations using the STEAR cycle.
- It is possible to have different thoughts and emotions about the same situation.

- Your results are impacted by the way you think, feel, and act.

5

Thoughts Trigger Emotions

What is a thought? Have you ever stopped to think about what a thought is and why we have them? It's funny when you think about it! We have thoughts all the time and most of them slip in and out of our minds all day long. In its most simple form, a thought is a sentence that occurs in the brain. What blows my mind is that the brain has anywhere from 50,000 – 70,000 thoughts per day, which breaks down to 35 – 48 thoughts per minute. Isn't that wild? As I became familiar with thought work and learned that our thoughts are what create our reality, I wanted to control the thoughts my brain was producing. I tried to stop it from creating one thought and tried to force it to think another thought. Unfortunately, you cannot tell your brain to stop thinking. You can meditate and learn to not perseverate on the thoughts that appear, but your brain does not have an off switch. The good news is that, although you cannot stop your brain from creating thoughts, you can learn to manage your thinking and train yourself to consider and believe new thoughts. This is the core of becoming emotionally fit.

Thoughts Vs. Belief Systems

Belief systems are thoughts you've rehearsed in your mind to the point they feel fundamentally true. Beliefs tend to be an overarching thought with several supporting thoughts that provide evidence for the primary belief. When you believe a thought to be truth, your brain creates a story around that thought. The story is a series of sentences that describe in detail the reasons why you believe this thought. Take the thought "Children learn by coming to school." If you believe this is true, you most likely have a series of other thoughts you believe that corroborate this belief, such as "Schools have trained educators." "Schools provide training in reading, writing, math, science, social studies, and the arts." "Kids would not have access to learning if they did not come to school."

Understanding the difference between beliefs and thoughts is crucial when it comes to your desire to feel better. A thought is neutral until you decide whether or not to believe it. Once you decide that a thought is true for you, your brain will kick into gear looking for all the evidence it can gather to support your decision to believe the thought is true.

Many of our belief systems are deeply rooted because they started from an early age. Our thoughts on topics like money, work, and spirituality were instilled before we started school. It is often these types of belief systems that are the most challenging to question. In order to change your life, you will have to be willing to change your belief systems. This will require you try on new beliefs, test drive them, and feel awkward during the process. You will have to be willing to feel emotions you most likely have been avoiding.

Vibrations Vs. Sensations

In order to better understand emotions, we need to decipher what they are. When we describe how an emotion feels, we notice they are basically a vibration in our bodies. This is why we call them feelings. A thought appears and our body responds to the thought through emotion. What we feel when we experience an emotion is a physical response to the thoughts occurring in our mind. An emotion starts with a thought that occurs in the brain and sends a message to the body. It is different than a body sensation. A body sensation is a message that the body sends to the brain. A sensation is the body's way of communicating needs. When your stomach growls because it is hungry, the growling is initiated in the stomach, which sends signals to your brain telling you to eat. It is involuntary in nature. Emotions, on the other hand, are determined when we give a certain meaning to our thoughts on a situation. The dictionary defines emotion as a mental state. This means that our emotions originate from our brain – our state of mind. A situation is always neutral until we give it meaning through the thoughts we think. When we believe a thought, it triggers either a positive or negative emotion. For example, whenever you are feeling worried, you are thinking and believing thoughts that something bad could or will happen.

When I talk about emotions, I will usually refer to them as positive emotions – emotions that feel good in your body (happy, excited, peaceful) – and negative emotions – emotions that do not feel good in your body (anger, fear, sadness, shame, embarrassment). There will also be times when you seem to feel neutral about a situation. My experience tells me that when I feel neutral about something, I am not attaching any significance to it. Either I do not have a thought about it or I do not believe a thought I am having about it. For instance, I have neutral feelings about your superintendent. I do not know her or him, I do not work for her or him, therefore I do not have any thoughts or emotions associated with her or him. My only connection to your superintendent that I am aware of is that she or he is a fellow human being and educator. Other than that, I have no feelings about her or him.

However, I'd put money down that you have thoughts, beliefs, opinions, and feelings about your superintendent. They may be highly positive, highly negative, or somewhere in the middle. The point is that, when you have a thought and you believe that thought to be true, your body will have an emotional response to the thought.

In order to get the most transformation out of the STEAR cycle, it is imperative to understand and believe that all emotions are caused by your thinking. The tricky part of getting your brain on board is that the cycle happens so quickly, it can be a challenge to see in the moment that it is a thought causing the emotion. Your brain is capable of creating several thoughts in rapid succession, each of which immediately triggers emotional responses in the body. Because this happens almost instantaneously, often times the emotional response is your first clue that you are attaching meaning to a thought. This is why understanding the STEAR cycle is so important. STEAR will help you slow down the process in order to analyze it one component at a time.

The first thing people want to do when they cognitively understand this concept is to do what I wanted to do, which is control their thoughts. We rationalize to ourselves, "Oh, if I am feeling negative emotion about this situation, then I just need to change the way I think about it." Unfortunately, it's not easy to thought swap most of the time. First of all, you cannot stop your brain from producing thoughts. That's one of its primary jobs. Your brain is so efficient at producing thoughts that it creates multiple thoughts around an issue in a very short amount of time. Where you might be able to think differently about one aspect of a situation, your brain is still creating other thoughts around the situation in an effort to protect you and show you evidence that its thoughts are true. I suggest starting with awareness. When a situation is bothering you in some form of negative emotion, start with writing down all of the thoughts that come up about it. Just list the thoughts and see which ones stand out the most to you. Once they are on paper, you can review them as an observer of your thinking. I also find it helpful to drop into my body and discern where the vibration is occurring in the body. Getting your brain and your body to connect while you act as an observer of both allows you to detach from the thought for a moment. Looking at your thoughts with curiosity and fascination instead of anxiety and control permits you to consider alternate thoughts that better serve you.

Client Case: Roxanne

Let's observe a situation one of my clients experienced and pretend that we have the ability to actually see her thoughts and emotions as she walks through this scenario. Roxanne has a teacher who struggles with classroom management. She cringes as she hears the chaos from down the hall and every time she enters the room, students are up from their seats, paper and materials are all over the floor, and the teacher is raising his voice to get the students' attention. She is so disturbed that she heads straight to her office. She walks down the hall with her jaw clenched, her fists balled up, stomping as she walks.

From her perspective, she believes the chaotic classroom is the cause of her negative emotional state. She also believes that if she could change that situation and improve his management style, she would feel better. She does not realize it is her thoughts about the chaotic classroom that are the triggering her emotional response. As the observers of her brain, we are able to see the string of thoughts that are appearing.

What is going on in there?

He cannot handle the students.

That room is total chaos!

There are no systems in place.

This is a mess.

I can't believe parents haven't complained.

He doesn't seem to implement the coach's suggestions.

I'm not even sure where to start with him.

We've had this conversation before.

I'm at my wit's end.

When you see the list of thoughts, it's no surprise that Roxanne's emotional state is highly agitated and frustrated. Her series of thoughts is popping into her brain and without realizing it, she is choosing to believe they are all true. Because she believes they are true, her body has a vibrational response that matches her beliefs. For most of us, the emotional response is the first thing we notice and because it's the first thing we notice, we connect the situation directly to the emotions. The thought "My thinking is causing me to feel agitated" does not surface. The other thoughts emerge at rapid fire and we sink into emotional reaction.

If we put ourselves into Roxanne's body and think about her situation, our brains are able to relate to her thoughts and we can literally create the same emotion by attaching the same meaning to the thoughts. Try it. Imagine the situation of the chaotic classroom. Think the thoughts she was thinking as you glance around the room. Notice how your body responds when you think these thoughts. You may grit your teeth and clench your jaw; you may feel tightness in your chest or maybe your stomach feels like it's been punched. However your body responds, the universal truth is this: When you believe a thought to be true and you do not like the thought, your body will physically respond in the form of a vibration to the negative emotion. The more intense the thought, the more intense the emotional response.

Why We Avoid Negative Emotion

We spend a great deal of time and energy trying to avoid negative vibrations. We tend to ignore, procrastinate, and distract ourselves because having to think about why we are frustrated is uncomfortable in the mind and the body. The reason we spend so much time and energy avoiding negative emotion is because emotional pain can feel as painful or worse than physical pain. However, the problem with avoiding negative feelings without observing the thought triggering the emotion is that nothing will change. In fact, not acknowledging the negative emotion will encourage it to linger and expand. Negative emotions are designed to get your attention. They are present to stimulate a desire for change.

Here's where irony comes into play. As humans, we are wired to seek pleasure and avoid pain. Our brain never wants us to feel pain or think painful thoughts because its job is to protect us at all times. Our brain cannot tell the difference between real danger and perceived danger so it is constantly working to protect you from any feelings of pain. It also cannot tell the difference between physical pain and emotional pain. To the brain, all pain is the same. Intense negative emotion feels incredibly painful in the body, so the brain wants to jump in and guard us from harm. Your brain will do everything in its power to guide you toward activities and thoughts that bring you happiness and guide you away from activities and thoughts that bring you pain and discomfort. This is why we find ourselves avoiding and resisting actions that our brain deems as painful, including thinking thoughts that trigger negative emotions.

The problem with this solution is that in order for us to learn, grow, and expand, we must go through discomfort. This is why people say that in order to grow, you must get out of your comfort zone. Think of the students at your school. Don't we tell them daily to take risks, try new things, publicly share their work, and persevere through testing and assignments? Expanding our knowledge and experiences requires emotional discomfort. It is our job to recognize that while emotional pain can cause intense vibrations, it does not cause true physical harm. Knowing this is how we can commit to difficult changes and allow ourselves to feel negative emotions during the process.

Summary

- Our brains have over 50,000 thoughts per day.
- We cannot turn off our brains from creating thoughts.
- We can decide whether or not we believe our thoughts are true.
- A series of thoughts we believe are true are called belief systems.
- Thoughts we believe are true trigger an emotional response.
- Our emotions are vibrations in our body.
- We are wired to avoid negative emotion.

6

Emotional State Impacts
Your Approach

Tony Robbins, a forefather in the self-development and coaching industry, says that our brain develops blueprints for our life circumstances. Blueprints are mental frameworks that specify how we believe our lives and the world should operate. They are the stories we create based on our personal set of expectations. When our life conditions – or the current reality of what is – align with our blueprints, we experience happiness and pleasure. When life conditions do not align with our blueprint expectations, we experience pain and suffering. This means that when things in our life are going the way we think they should be going, we feel happy. When things in our life are not going the way we believe they should, we feel discontent.

The way we approach life when we feel happy is different than the way we approach it when we feel unhappy. My definition of approach is the set of actions we take based on our emotional state. Our emotional state of being directly impacts the way we choose to handle ourselves. Think how you approach your day when you are bubbling with enthusiasm and energy versus how you approach your day when you are tired and dreading your day. Do you take the same actions throughout the day, no matter how you are feeling? Most people do not. They allow their emotional state to determine their behavior.

Before I learned this concept through self-coaching, I was letting my emotions drive my entire life. I did not comprehend that I had some control over how I was feeling or that my emotions impacted my approach to daily situations. I simply reacted to the emotional state I was in at the time. When you believe your life is a product of outside circumstances, you become a puppet of your unmanaged thoughts and emotions. This leads to inconsistent results in your life because you will choose how you approach a situation based on your mood in the moment. Considering how often our moods fluctuate throughout any given day, letting our emotions dictate our approach toward our life goals seems risky.

When I was hired for my first principalship, I was so excited about the new job. I had prepared for over two years, earning my administrative credential, taking workshops on school leadership, reading books, and talking to veteran principals. I ached to become a principal. When I stepped into my new role, I had a very rose-colored blueprint of what the job would entail. I imagined myself knowing every student on campus by name, grade, classroom, and personal interests. I thought I would connect closely with my staff and community, improve school-wide procedures, handle my paperwork and appointments with time to spare, and skyrocket student achievement. To my dismay, the reality of my life conditions definitely did not align with my blueprint of how I envisioned the job. I laugh now thinking back on that time of life because I can see the dissonance, but I can assure you I was not laughing then. I experienced an incredible amount of angst because my blueprint did not match my reality. Being in a constant state of angst led me to spend my work day reacting to situations as they arose versus approaching my career with intentional, planned, action steps.

The Three Approaches

When we experience negative emotion, we choose one of three approaches based on that emotion:

- Stall in Inaction
- Indulge in Reaction
- Create Intentional Action

Stall in Inaction

When we stall in inaction, we do not take any type of action based on our negative feelings about the situation. We ignore and avoid action because we either are unwilling to do the work or we are afraid of experiencing further negative feelings. For instance, if your district policy is that each school sends out a weekly newsletter and you believe that it's not worth your time, you can decide not to write the newsletter (inaction). Your choice to not write the letter stems from your belief that it's not worth your time and you don't want to put forth the effort because doing so would cause you more pain. Although you run the risk of having to answer to your colleagues or superiors when you choose not to take action, you may decide that their feedback is potentially less painful than writing the newsletter.

On the other hand, you may stall in inaction from the belief that you don't know how or what to write about in the newsletter. This inaction is slightly different in the sense that it's coming from a state of confusion versus anger. This happens to new principals quite often. We are asked to take on a task and then sit idle because we believe we don't know how to complete it. How many times have you been asked to learn a new application or program when you dread technology or been required to present to the school board when you hate public speaking? We may procrastinate working on these tasks because we believe that doing so will cause us discomfort. Instead of setting aside some time to learn the program or write the presentation, we find ourselves avoiding the work by saying we don't know how and don't have time.

I want to point out that stalling in inaction is different than intentionally choosing not to take action. Let's say you've received invitations to sit on three different steering committees for your district. You are thrilled to serve on two of them, but the third one just doesn't float your boat nor do you want to spread yourself too thin. Intentionally deciding to not take action by not being on all three committees is an empowered decision. It comes from a place of understanding your boundaries and selectively choosing what actions are a best fit for you. Stalling is when you attempt to avoid further negative emotions; intentionally choosing inaction is when you proactively decide that not taking action is your best choice.

Indulge in Reaction

When we indulge in reacting, we are letting our emotions take the wheel. We deflect, blame, resist, and justify ourselves. We blame the situation or other people for our feelings and actions. We disagree with what happened, often hashing it over in our minds time and time again. We lash out at others and spend time trying to explain and justify our thinking. This type of approach feels the most disempowered because it stems from the belief that something outside of our control is making us feel and act a particular way.

Let's look back at the newsletter scenario. If you are acting in reaction, you are in some way blaming your emotions on other people. You may be thinking that very few people read newsletter so why write it, or you may be thinking that your boss should not be asking you to spend your time as a school leader this way. Whenever you are responding to a situation where you believe something outside of you is the cause of your emotions, you are indulging in reaction.

Create Intentional Action

The issue that arises when we allow negative emotions to select our approach to a situation, through either inaction or reaction, is that we experience inconsistent results. The actions we take or do not take when we let anger, frustration, disappointment, sadness, resentment, and vengeance decide for us are vastly different than when we consciously choose to act. And while this cycle creates disappointing results, the larger tragedy is that both of these approaches strip you of your personal power. When you blame situations for your emotions and actions, you are disempowering yourself. You are giving up your right to feel and act the way you want. You are telling yourself that other people make you feel and behave a certain way and that you don't have control over it.

You cannot lead a school or your life from a place of disempowerment. Your professional and personal life is your responsibility and you are here because you are more than ready to own your emotions and actions.

The way you take back your power is by creating intentional action. What this means is that you become conscious of your thoughts and you intentionally choose thoughts that create the emotions and determine the approach that you would like to take. You take ownership of your emotions versus blaming outside circumstances. You proactively decide how you want to show up in the world ahead of time so you can select a set of actions that aligns with what kind of school leader you want to be.

Back to our newsletter example, an intentional action might be to schedule one hour a month where you write all four weeks' worth of newsletters and hand it over to your secretary so she can format the rest of the newsletter. You could also find articles online instead of taking time to write them yourself, or perhaps you find someone else who is happy to write the newsletter. When you decide to intentionally choose to take action, a number of options become available and the task gets completed in a way that works best for you.

Don't Worry, Be Happy?

I bet you are wondering if this means you need to feel happy in order to take intentional action. It seems that negative emotions correlate to negative approaches and positive emotions lead to positive approaches. Here's the secret most people don't know: You don't have to feel happy in order to choose intentional action. Even when you have negative feelings, you can acknowledge your feelings, and consciously choose to plan out an intentional approach and take action. The difference between reacting from a state of negativity and intentionally choosing an approach even though you do not like how you are feeling is resisting feeling the emotion versus allowing the emotion to be present while you are in action.

Think of a time you were asked to do something at work that you really did not want to do – let's say public speaking. The director of curriculum has asked all of the principals to present the new math curriculum at a town hall community meeting. You are brand new in your position and you really hate speaking in front of large groups. When you are in resistance, you might complain, pout, and blame the director for making such a ludicrous request. You may even get someone else to present for you.

The actions you take in resistance are to avoid feeling the burn of public speaking. You are in resistance any time you avoid feeling the negative emotion you anticipate will occur if you take a certain approach. When you take intentional action despite your fear of feeling the fear, you allow yourself to feel scared while you are giving the speech. You don't back down from the fear of speaking.

The funny thing about resisting negative emotion is that in our efforts to avoid feeling afraid, we feel anger and resentment. Either way, we feel badly, but when we resist, we choose an approach that avoids the original emotion and replaces it with a buffering emotion. We are more willing to feel anger than fear. The brain will avoid fear at all costs, even at the expense of feeling disgruntled. This does not serve our greater purpose in the long run because if we allow our brain to talk us out of all fear, we will not advance in our lives. We would not engage in any action that our brain deems as physically or emotionally dangerous. However, if our brain's assessment of danger was always accurate, we would not exist as a species. We would not have learned to walk, try new foods, ride a bike, drive a car, move away from home, accept our first job, get married, or have children.

So why it is that we are willing to approach some situations that feel risky and others we do everything within our power to avoid? How is it that we devoted four or more years to studying education, potentially taking on significant debt in the process, took countless exams to obtain our teaching credentials, interviewed in the face of being rejected, accepted our first teaching positions, and stepped in front of 25 – 30 children we did not know?

We did it again when we decided to become school administrators. We took classes, paid for our master's degree, took the credentialing test, interviewed, got rejected, and finally left our classroom to take the helm of our first school. The answer is this: We had a compelling reason. We dedicated our time, money, and effort because we felt compelled to lead. The calling to lead moved us more than our disdain for exams, our sadness in leaving the classroom, our interview anxiety, and our fear of public criticism. This is how I know that it is possible to take intentional action in the face of feeling negative emotion.

Your job is to use your emotions as an indicator to what approach you are about to choose. Notice situations at work that stimulate fear or anger in you. When you are feeling these emotions, what approach does your brain want to take? Does it try to convince you to avoid taking action? Does it want to explode in reaction? Just observe the thoughts that come up as you are feeling the fear or anger. Right now as I write, I am observing my own emotions and noticing the thoughts that are triggering them. It's a beautiful Sunday morning. My husband is golfing at Spanish Bay with colleagues, and I am inside working on my book. My thoughts causing me pain sound like this: "I don't want to be indoors writing my book." "I want to be out having fun." "This book is taking all of my time." "I'm tired of writing under such tight deadlines." This string of consciousness arouses resistance. I want to stop writing (inaction). If I choose this approach, this chapter will not get written. I've decided to observe all the thoughts in my head and tell my brain, "I hear ya. I want to go play in the sun too. The book will be done in four more weeks and then you can take some down time for fun while celebrating this massive accomplishment. Let's stick with it for now so we can dance in delight in June." I am choosing intentional action despite feeling resistance. I am allowing the resistance to be present in my body as I am typing. I look out the window at the blue sky and feel the sadness in my chest as I dream of walking down to the beach.

The key to achieving what you want is to be willing to allow yourself to feel negative emotions. Just as I am feeling sad about not getting what I want in this moment, you can tolerate any emotion. Your brain will tell you otherwise, but you can withstand discomfort, angst, fear, anger, desire, and urges.

Knowing this is simple, but it is not easy. One way to help your brain relax is to find a compelling reason in allowing the negative emotion to be present. Back to the public speaking example, if you are deathly afraid to get up and speak, can you find any compelling reason for following through even though you are scared? Perhaps you can give yourself something to look forward to after the event. Maybe you want to be a role model to your students by showing them how to be scared and try something new. Giving your brain a compelling reason to do something it fears is like holding the back of your toddler's bike as he takes the training wheels off for the first time. Give your brain a hand to lower its fear and before you know it, you'll be riding on your own in no time.

Summary

- Blueprints are one way your brain develops expectations for your life circumstances.
- If our expectations align with our life, we are happy.
- If our expectations do not align with our life, we are unhappy.
- The way we approach our life varies based on our emotional state.
- Negative emotion triggers inaction, reaction, or intentional action.
- It is possible to feel negative emotion and take positive action.

7

Our Approach Influences Our Results

We're on the last component of the STEAR model – our results. This is the component that gets the most attention before we understand that, in fact, it is the most influenced by all of the other components. Our brain ignores our thoughts and emotions and dives right into action and results. This makes sense because our results are the physical manifestation of our thoughts, emotions, and actions. They are tangible to the brain. The brain likes to focus on our results because it does not want to experience the discomfort of the interior work that takes place prior to taking action.

We believe that taking action is what creates uncomfortable feelings. We think that the act of making a phone call to an upset parent is why we feel resistant. However, the reason we feel resistant does not come from taking the action of picking up the phone, dialing the number, and talking to another person. These are all harmless actions. None of these actions will cause you pain. The feeling of resistance comes from the thought that the conversation will not go well.

So before we've taken action, our brain has anticipated what the emotion the body will experience. This anticipated outcome determines whether or not we make the phone call and from what state of emotion we communicate with the parent. What we believe will be the result of the phone call steers the way we approach the call and ultimately determines the result of that phone conversation. If you approach the parent from a state of fear, you may come across sounding like an incompetent pushover. If you approach the parent from a state of frustration, the conversation may result in a heated discussion met with resentment and defensiveness. If you make the phone call from the emotional state of compassion and assurance, you may find yourself in a pleasant exchange with the parent. However you choose to approach the phone call will impact the outcome.

I think most people can wrap their heads around that. Where we go astray is by not fully believing that we can choose our approach, regardless of our emotional state and that we can shift our emotional state by shifting the thoughts we think.

When we are leading schools, we are bombarded with situation after situation. On any given day, principals deal with tardy students, double-booked meetings, angry parents, field trip hiccups, not enough substitute teachers, fighting children, budget cuts, failed technology, state testing, recess and lunch duty, bandage distribution, fire drills, and school assembly coordination. And these are what come up before we check our 200 emails! We make hundreds of decisions on a moment's notice. For each situation that occurs, thoughts appear. Because the brain generates thoughts with or without or conscious consent, we believe that we cannot control our thoughts. When I use the word control, I do not mean that you have power over whether the brain creates thoughts. I mean that you have power in deciding if you are going to believe a particular thought.

The enlightened Byron Katie suggests that we question all thoughts. A thought appears. Is it true? If you believe it's true, can you absolutely know 100% that it is true? We often believe our thoughts as facts when most of the time they are opinions we've come to believe as true facts. When we believe our thoughts are facts of reality, then we have no means to change the thought. If, however, we are willing to question whether a thought is true, we gain the ability to study it, test it, and decide if the thought is one we want to keep or dismiss.

What we tend to focus on in lieu of studying our thoughts is the action required to get a desired result. As a school leader, you have an agenda of what you'd like to accomplish at your school site. You most likely are also trying to accomplish the requested results of your boss or school board. We look at this list of results and wonder what approach we need to take in order to achieve these results. We spend a great deal of time planning our approach and taking massive action with the hope that all of our efforts will create the result we want. We insist that the way to achieve results is to stay in a constant state of action. What we don't often take into consideration is the rationale behind the action or the energy driving the action.

Client Case: Sadie

My client Sadie says that she is inundated with action. She flies from her office to classrooms to the lunchroom to the playground and back to her office. She feels like she is in meetings for most of her day and when she's not in a meeting, she is scheduling meetings or preparing for meetings. Her evenings consist of email responses regarding follow-ups to past meetings and answering questions for upcoming meeting agendas.

Can you relate? She feels like she is in constant motion and she truly believes that her high energy and high visibility approach will positively impact her and her boss's desired results.

This may be true to an extent, however, when she describes her emotional state she says she feels exhausted and unaccomplished. She does not feel like she ever gets to all the things she is supposed to do and that no amount of time is enough to complete all she wants to get done.

What she had not considered before coaching was what beliefs she was holding onto that drove her actions. We explored questions such as, "Why am I so busy? What am I actually accomplishing? Is my approach to my job achieving the results I want? Is there a better way to approach this job and feel less overwhelm and exhaustion?" Through this exploration, Sadie was able to decipher when she was taking action based on the thought she should do something versus choosing actions that she felt were the most effective for her students, staff, and herself.

Confirmation Bias

When I reflect back to my first years, I can relate to Sadie's story and see how I too credited my busy-ness for some of our successes as a school. The thoughts behind all of this action were "Good principals are active principals. They are enthusiastic, energetic, connected, and engaged." I believed this to be true, so I approached the job with high energy and high involvement and was able to achieve many of the results I'd set for myself. However, what I did at a subconscious level was focus on what was going well and continue to take consistent action toward those results and inadvertently ignore the results that I was not achieving. Our brains do this all the time. It's called confirmation bias. The brain seeks out evidence to reinforce the belief we want to believe is true and filters out any information or thoughts that contradict our belief system. I was reinforcing my belief that being a busy principal meant I was a good principal and ignoring data that put my approach into question.

Confirmation bias makes it incredibly challenging to see how we might be sabotaging our own efforts. When our brain holds tightly to a belief, it creates a powerful argument, which in our mind turns an opinion we have into a fact. My approach to my job to me sounded like simple truth. I thought that if I continued to be really involved in as much as I could on campus, kids and teachers would thrive, parents would be happy, and test scores would continue to grow. My brain found plenty of evidence to show me how this could be true, so I never questioned it. I did not ask myself questions that challenged my theory. Was it true that all kids and teachers were thriving? Was it true that all parents were happy? Was it true that test scores for all students continued to grow? You can imagine the answers to these questions. You can also imagine how continuing to believe that my approach was working allowed me to indulge in maintaining the status quo. It allowed me to be nestled in my comfort zone by not having to feel the intensity of emotions that these questions raised for me as a school leader.

Results are always happening regardless of our approach. We cannot know whether or not an approach is working if we are not monitoring our thoughts and emotions behind the approach. Remember, our thoughts about our situation trigger an emotion. Our emotions drive the way we decide to approach our situation. From this emotional state, we deploy an action step or set of actions. This is critical to understand because of its impact on our results.

Depending on your emotional state, you choose a plan of action. You either indulge in reaction, stall in inaction, or create intentional action. For many of us, most of the time we have little or no awareness of our emotional state, so we tend to react. The emotions appear and we respond according to how we are feeling. We all do this. It is normal to react because the process happens so quickly. We also might lean into reaction when the emotions are incredibly intense one way or the other. Strong emotions feel more challenging to observe than less intense emotions. For example, you are more likely to react if you witness a student being attacked on the playground than you would be when you are checking your morning emails (although I have had emails that make me want to lose my mind!). Generally speaking, the higher the intensity of your emotional state, the more likely you are to engage in reacting.

On the other hand, when our emotional state is very relaxed or apathetic, we may choose to do nothing. We brush things off, we procrastinate, and we avoid taking action. It can be a very powerful choice not to react. I often consider inaction over reaction, for a short period of time, so I can make a plan for intentional action. What is important to know is that inaction is a form of taking action. You do get a result from the act of inaction. Results are always occurring, regardless of which approach you choose.

Here is what I find absolutely fascinating about the way we think. We believe that our results impact the way we feel which impacts the way we think. The reverse is actually true. How we think impacts our emotions and our emotions impact our results. What is so cool about understanding this is that if you focus on obtaining the result with unwavering commitment, you will be willing to stay in an emotional state that will allow you to endure questioning your approach and trying multiple approaches until you reach the goal. This happens because when you are willing to achieve a result no matter what, the thoughts you in your mind are things like, "I will try multiple ways to solve this problem," "I know I can do this," "I'm committed to questioning my approach," "There is always a solution." These thoughts lead to emotions such as capable, determined, and energetic which drive you toward all the potential approaches to get you what you want.

Summary

- The way we choose to approach any situation influences the outcome.
- We often assume that the situation is the cause of our results.
- It is possible to question the thoughts we believe are true.
- When we believe our thoughts without question, we seek evidence to support our beliefs. This is called confirmation bias.
- Results are always occurring, regardless of which approach you choose.
- You can alter your results by adjusting your approach.

8

You Got It All Wrong Kid

N ow that you know the components of the STEAR cycle, we can start to tackle applying it to situations in your workday. From a cognitive standpoint, it would seem that you could simply run a STEAR cycle on any situation where you feel a negative emotion and replace your thoughts or your approach and feel better. Unfortunately, our brains do not let us off the hook that easily. Our brains will sniff out some level of danger in most situations and generate a feeling of fear that feels very real to us.

This flight or fight response occurs in the reptilian portion of our brain. The oldest of the three parts, the reptilian brain is responsible for our basic instincts and bodily functions, such as our heartbeat, our breathing, and our visceral response to danger, which stimulates the feeling of fear. Fear occurs as an impulsive reaction because it was designed to keep us from being eaten by lions, tigers, and bears. It would seem that reacting to our fear is not controllable within our neocortex, which is the part of our brain where our ability to reason occurs.

Now that our brains have evolved and we better understand how they function, we can learn to distinguish fear of bodily destruction from emotional and mental fears. It's important to keep in mind that although fear-based emotions trigger an intense desire to flee from situations, the emotional vibrations you feel when you are scared cannot physically hurt you. In the next few chapters, we are going to look at three basic human fears and train our brain to explore new ways of thinking that will move us closer to achieving any result that we want.

Why We Fear Being Wrong

One of our deepest fears as humans is to be wrong. Most of us cannot tolerate the emotions associated with being told we are wrong or we are doing something wrong. This is understandable because being wrong is often associated with feelings of shame. Brené Brown, author and researcher on shame and vulnerability, defines shame as "the intensely painful feeling or experience of believing that we are flawed and therefore unworthy of love and belonging."

Shame can be an overwhelmingly painful feeling because it is deeply rooted into our belief systems from an early age. Most of us can think back to a time early in our lives when we felt shamed by another person, usually an adult that we loved, adored, and trusted like our parents or a teacher. As young children, our families tell us what behaviors are right and wrong. In school, we are taught that there is a right way and a wrong way. As adults, we learn that it is wrong to be wrong and that you are rewarded only when you are right.

These social conditioning lessons are helpful as we are learning how to engage with others in our society, and they also develop people-pleasers and conformists. How you interpreted these lessons is what drives how you feel about yourself when you do something labeled as wrong. Common thoughts around being wrong include: I am a bad person. I do bad things. It's bad to be wrong. I need to do what's right. Right is good, wrong is bad.

As adults, we hold onto these lessons and memories. Recollections of past experiences can bring up intense pain. What we must realize is that these emotions are based on something that is not happening to us in this moment. We are recreating the feelings by reliving the memory. Whenever we remember past pain or anticipate future pain, we create unnecessary suffering in the present moment. This suffering based on your past pain or anticipated pain in your future does not help you live an empowered life. Being afraid of being labeled as wrong stalls your progress and stifles you from showing up authentically as you.

How We Avoid Being Wrong

Because being wrong feels so awful, our brains are trained experts in finding ways to step around being wrong. The easiest way to avoid being wrong is to admit right off the bat that we don't know how to do something. When we say we don't know how, we are really saying that we are afraid we'll take action and someone will tell us it's wrong or we won't get the result we want. Not knowing how is a way of not having to take action and try something new. It is indulgent in the sense that it gives you permission to not face your fear of doing it wrong.

You must call yourself out whenever you find yourself saying you don't know how to do a task. The truth is that you do not ever know how to do something until you have actually done it. Nobody knows how to drive a car until they get behind the wheel and drive. Nobody knows how to be a principal until they get hired and go to work as a principal.

The same is true when we say we are confused or overwhelmed. When we say these things to ourselves, we are saying that we don't know how to get started or that we don't know how to handle the situations in our lives. Not knowing how, confusion, and overwhelm never serve you. They are not situations. They are not facts that can be upheld in a court of law. They are your opinion of your situation – your thoughts about your situation. Your thoughts that you don't know, or you are confused, or that you are overwhelmed create feelings of confusion and overwhelm. You create not knowing how, confusion, and overwhelm in your brain as a mechanism to avoid the emotions you associate with being wrong or doing it wrong.

Wrong Is an Opinion

If you look up wrong in the dictionary, its definition is a series of statements that are of opinion in nature: "not in accordance with what is morally right or good; deviating from the truth or fact; not correct in action, judgment, opinion, method, etc.; not proper or usual; out of order; not suitable or appropriate". This leads me to believe that what is wrong is simply an opinion. There is no absolute right or wrong way. So if there is no absolute right or wrong way to do something, why are we so afraid of doing it wrong?

Our society has a system of thoughts that collectively we believe are true. They feel like facts because our society has collected information, written theories, and instituted laws that define right and wrong. But, what has been determined as wrongful is based on an opinion of other people. You can argue that something as serious as killing another person is wrong because it is illegal and immoral. That is your opinion. People's opinion about whether killing is right or wrong does not deter all people from killing other people. Furthermore, the fact that there is a law against killing another human does not eliminate all killing in our country. What about the person who does the killing? Would they necessarily agree that killing is wrong? What about the death penalty? If the idea that killing is wrong was 100 percent fact, then the death penalty could not exist and wars would not occur. I use this extreme example to point out thoughts that are universally agreed upon, such as "It is wrong to take the life of another person," feel like truth, yet they are only thoughts. They are strongly rooted belief systems in the majority of individuals which supports our belief that the thought is true, but the fact is that people kill. Whether it is determined to be right or wrong is in the opinion of others.

I remember listening to one of Byron Katie's books on CD, before books were available on our phones (I am dating myself). She told a story about the first time she heard someone say "Namaste." She thought they were saying, "No mistakes." She loved this concept and chooses to believe that nothing wrong ever happens. I agree with her and invite you to consider trying on this thought for yourself. Everything happens for a reason, even things you consider wrong. The reality is that they happened, so it was not wrong. It may not be what you wanted, but it happened in order for you to know what you want versus what you don't want.

If you can wrap your head around the idea that wrong is an opinion, then it will allow you to start questioning the thoughts you have about what is right and wrong. For example, many leaders are afraid to be decisive. They stall in indecisiveness because they are afraid of making a wrong decision. When faced with a decision, ask yourself the following questions. These questions will expose the thoughts your brain is producing around making decisions and the fear of being wrong.

- What would making the wrong decision mean?
- Who is saying the decision is wrong?
- Why is the decision wrong?
- What should you decide instead?
- What will happen if you make a wrong decision?
- Why is that so bad?

See if these questions help reduce the fearful feelings of being wrong and allow you to explore the facts of what the decision will actually mean instead of allowing the fears to show up without question and influence your decision-making as a leader.

Asking for Help

When you want to learn how to do something, it is absolutely acceptable to ask for help. This is a brilliant time hack. Why take the time to learn something through trial and error if you have access to someone who is proficient at the task? Specifically, if you are a new leader, it is so helpful to take advantage of being new. People are generally very kind when you are new to a position and are eager to learn from them. They want to help and they want to see you succeed.

Asking for help to point you in the right direction and get you started or when you get stuck is highly recommended. Asking for help with the intention of someone else doing the work for you is not. There is a difference between asking how to do something every step of the way to avoid making a mistake and feeling you've done it wrong and asking for support and guidance so that you get started and take action. When asking for help, be clear that you are asking with the intention of learning so that you can take action.

How to Combat Fear of Doing it Wrong

First of all, know there is no wrong. Nothing you do is wrong or bad. You are not wrong. You are not bad. Your decisions are not wrong or bad. Your results are not wrong or bad. They may not be the results you wanted, but they do not mean anything has gone wrong. Also know that other people's opinion that you are wrong does not need to mean anything about you. Remind yourself that their opinion is their correct way and your opinion is your correct way.

You can use the STEAR model when you are presented with a task that is new to you. You can start by deciding what is it that you want to accomplish. Write the outcome you want in the Results line. Then jump to how it would feel to accomplish that result. Write down the emotional state you will be in if you successfully accomplish your task. When you are in this emotional state, how do you approach the task at hand? This approach is how you start taking action and stop worrying about being wrong. Let's say you are asked to prepare a budget update for the PTA meeting using Excel, and you have never used Excel. You can run a STEAR model.

S = Request for budget update using Excel

T =

_____

_____

E =

_____

_____

A =

_____

_____

R = Create budget update using Excel

S = Request for budget update using Excel

T =
_____

_____

E = Competent

A =
_____

_____

R = Create budget update using Excel

S = Request for budget update using Excel

T =
_____

_____

E = Competent

A = Ask my secretary to guide me, review other Excel reports, play around on Excel, schedule time to complete the update, ask for help when I get stuck

R = Create budget update using Excel

S = Request for budget update using Excel

T = I am capable of learning Excel.

E = Competent

A = Ask my secretary to guide me, review other Excel reports, play around on Excel, schedule time to complete the update, ask for help when I get stuck

R = Create budget update using Excel

If you are having trouble identifying your emotional state and approach, you can drop out of your head and into your body. Close your eyes. Take a few deep breaths. Now ask yourself: What if you did know how? Where would you start? What if you weren't confused? Envision yourself going through the motions of completing the task with no confusion. Ask, if I was the person who knew how to do this, where would I start? What is one step I can take toward this goal? Write down whatever comes to mind. Then start taking action.

When we are new at something and we believe there is a right way and a wrong way, we think that we need confidence in order to make decisions and take action. We think that having confidence in our decision will bring us more certainty and avoid being wrong. What builds your confidence is not certainty. What builds your confidence is commitment and courage. You must commit to a decision and be courageous enough take action, even if you or someone else tells you it's wrong. Be willing to experience feelings of being wrong. Even though there is no such thing as wrong, you will continue to get feedback from your brain and others that you are wrong. That's ok. You can handle being wrong.

Summary
- The fear of being wrong is a universal human fear.
- We feel shame, guilt, and embarrassment when we believe we are wrong.
- We avoid being wrong through confusion, overwhelm, and saying we don't know how.

- There is no wrong. Wrong is always an opinion.
- Ask for help to keep you in taking action mode.
- Use the STEAR cycle to help you shift thoughts about what it means to be wrong.

9

That Is Socially Unacceptable

Being criticized, especially in a public forum, is another universal fear we experience as a social being. Nobody enjoys being criticized. In the education world, we call it "feedback." We say feedback to encapsulate both positive and negative comments, but we all know that our brain gravitates to the negative feedback, which is why I'm naming it criticism.

Even when criticism is given in private, our brain recoils and our defenses go up. Most individuals steer around criticism whenever possible in an attempt to avoid the force with which it strikes our mental state. When it does cross our path – and it will – if we aren't emotionally fit, criticism will leave deep cuts of pain, shame, and guilt. It deters us from authenticity and vulnerability, which means we will not be showing up as the leaders we want to be at work and in our lives.

Let's break down what criticism is so we can examine its components and find a savvy way to handle our emotions around criticism. The dictionary defines criticism as the act of passing judgment as to the merits of anything. When I read this, my brain immediately interpreted this definition as negative. The word judgment is used to define criticism, which is another word we label as harsh and negative. We correlate being judged and receiving criticism as a negative experience due to our memories of past experiences. We have all been criticized at some point. When we think back to those moments, we again experience the painful feelings we link to those moments. We develop a belief system that solidifies criticism as the enemy by making it mean we are not enough of something, and when we are not enough of something, we feel flawed.

Our brain, whose job is to protect us from harm, automatically goes into defense mode when it senses that a situation might result in judgment and criticism. Notice that this occurs only when we believe the criticism is true. This is important to distinguish. If someone were to tell you that you are terrible at walking, you would probably laugh and not think anything of it. You don't take the criticism seriously because you don't believe it and you don't make it mean anything. If someone yells at you during a principal's coffee and tells you that you suck (yes, this happened to me), and a part of you believes that you do suck, you will experience distress in that moment.

One emotional response to criticism lands us somewhere on the anger spectrum. When angry emotions are stirred, we tend to react. We put up our shields to deflect and defend ourselves. We want to fight and lash back. We try to explain and justify our decisions.

Another approach we slip into is inaction. We avoid putting ourselves out in front of others. We stop being willing to be authentic and vulnerable. These emotions fall in the sad range. We feel sorry for ourselves, beat ourselves up, or feel regret. Unfortunately, none of these approaches serve you for the better. The reason we respond to criticism this way is because our brain makes it mean that something is wrong with us and that we must change what we are doing or stop our work.

It is when we are unsure of ourselves and unresolved in our decisions that we believe other people's judgments of us. When we value other people's opinion over our own, we fall into the trap of people-pleasing. You do not want to fall into this rabbit hole. You must find the courage to value your opinion of yourself and of your decisions over any other person's opinion. Think of it this way, if people were supposed to value their critics over themselves, they would spend their entire lives trying to change who they are and would never create and put their work into the world. We'd have no art, no music, no books, and no Internet! If Steve Jobs had followed the advice of his critics and stopped creating, you would not be reading this book on your iPhone or iPad or MacBook through your Kindle App. Now wouldn't that have been a disservice to the world?

Making decisions about your career feels scary when you are afraid of receiving any kind of criticism. If you are contemplating the decision of staying in your job and being unhappy versus leaving the job and living with uncertainty and you share this decision with others, you will most certainly receive some level of criticism. Some people want you to stay. Others will tell you to go. They may be harsh with their words. "Are you crazy? You earned this position! You are the boss of a school, you have amazing benefits, and you make a ton of money. You'll regret leaving before your pension is at its peak. You only have 20 more years to go. You'd be stupid to quit now." Before you take this feedback into account and make any decision at all, let's figure out how to deal with the critics.

Handling Criticism

When we talk about being judged by other people, we are referring to their opinions about what we do or say. We tend to believe that if we act a certain way or say the right things, people will like us. If this were true, there would be no difference of opinion. Life would be all or none. All people would either like you or not like you. There would be only one right way to live. It would also mean that other people control your thoughts about them – that their actions and words make you feel a certain way about them. When you believe you can influence other people's thoughts about you, you disempower yourself. Deciding that people's opinions are nothing more than a reflection of themselves and that they have nothing to do with you gives you the freedom to go all in on your life and live exactly how you want to live.

My number one hack for handling criticism is to remember this: criticism is just an opinion. It is not fact. It is not a law of nature. It is one person's thought about a situation. The situation is your work. They have a thought about your work, which stimulates an emotional response within them. They choose to approach the situation (your work) by sharing their opinion of it. The result they are looking for is for you to accept their opinion and change your work in some way. The good news is that nobody gets to tell you how to think or feel. You get to decide how you will respond to another person's opinion of your work. This is the moment you can choose to step into your full power. Use these questions to help you determine your response:

- Are you having a strong emotional response? If so, why?
- What is your thought about the criticism?
- Is the criticism wrong or right in your mind?
- Does any part of the criticism resonate with you?
- Where's the nugget of truth? Does something ring true for you?

Observing your internal response to the criticism is an important part in choosing your approach. You need to determine what part of the criticism is triggering your emotions so you can question whether the comment rings true for you. If it does not, you can dismiss it. If it does, or a part of it does, then you can explore what your brain is making it mean about you and choose whether you want to change your thinking or change your approach.

Never have we lived in a time when it has been so easy to criticize others. Social media has created an entirely new way for folks to be brutal with their criticism *and* do it anonymously. They will say painful things about you, your loved ones, and your work. It stings.

But in the end, all criticism is simply an opinion. The reasons criticism stings are when we highly value the person's opinion who's given the criticism or we choose to believe it means something is wrong with us or what we are doing. Valuing someone else's opinion is fine if you are taking the criticism as constructive feedback to adjust your approach. It's when we value their opinion over our own that we give away our power and live by other people's standards.

You have courageously put yourself out in the world in a big way. Being a school leader is a target for public criticism. I commend you for being exposed and vulnerable. If you take anything away from this chapter, remember this: Criticism is always about the person who's giving it. It is a mirror of their thoughts. It's an opinion based from their lens of the world. It's how they are choosing to show up in the world. It's not about you or your work. It's how they view your work. It is simply an opinion. It doesn't have to mean anything more than that. The opinion to be most worried about is your own.

Take this book, for example. I loved creating this book for you. I did my best to provide you with thought-provoking content and contextualize it in a way that is easy to understand and digest. Some people will be into it; others will not. That's ok. Some people will love it; others won't. Either way, I'm good. I'd rather have taken the risk of some people not liking it than being afraid of not being liked, therefore never creating it, and being left wondering who could have been positively impacted had I been brave enough to handle my critics. You can care about other human beings without caring about their opinion. You don't need to change who you are or the work you do.

Make criticism mean it's about them and not you. It's the difference between empowerment and disenfranchisement. Now get out there and show the world what you've got!

Summary

- Criticism hurts because we make it mean we are not enough.
- When we believe the criticism, we react or slip into inaction.
- Criticism is just an opinion. You can take it or leave it
- Decide whether you believe the criticism or not.
- Adjust your approach as needed, but keep taking action!

10

The F Word

The word we perfectionists hate the most … Failure. What an ugly word! We want to think that none of us are failures, yet we spend so much time worrying that we will fail. We abstain from taking any action because we are afraid to fail. The thought of failing takes up a lot of our brain energy and it deters us from trying things we want to experience in our lives. The fear of failure is so prevalent that most people would rather not try at all than try and fail. Because of failure's power over us, we need to dig deeper into what it really is and why it feels so unnerving. Let's start with how failure is described and then we'll deconstruct it so we can manage our thoughts and emotions around the idea of failing.

When we talk about failure, we most often view it as a lack of success or being insufficient in some capacity. But what does that really mean? If you look at failure as a lack of success, how is a lack of success measured? What does being insufficient look like? How do you know if you've failed or not? What happens when we fail? The reason these questions arise when we attempt to define failure is because failure is composed in the mind. The definition of failure is in the eye of the beholder. We only fail when we have decided that we have failed.

Suppose you set out to run your first marathon. You're not exactly the athletic type, but a friend asked you to join her. The two of you pay to participate in training sessions for beginning runners. You work your buns off training for this race. You've spent hours building up your endurance. The big day comes and you and your friend cross the start line. It's been tough, but things are looking great and you are feeling so proud of yourself. You are only a mile from the finish line when you stumble and twist your ankle. Your friend rushes over to you and helps you up. You aren't able to run but you can hobble. She assists you to the medical tent where you get the attention you need. You never got to cross the finish line. Was this a failure?

The answer is that it depends. It depends on who is defining the success or failure. The organization that coordinated the race may say you failed because you technically did not cross the line. Other runners may agree. Even your friend may feel sad that you did not get to finish the race. But what about you? How do you define this moment for yourself? Was it a failure because you did not cross the finish line or was it a huge success because you achieved something beyond what you thought you were capable of doing? Your feelings of joy or sorrow over the race will be determined by what you make the situation mean for you.

Other people cannot define our failures. They can say that you've failed, but unless you also believe you have failed, their message has no merit. Their thought that we have failed is simply an opinion.

If we define what failure means for ourselves, then why are we so ghastly afraid of failing? I'm sure you are catching onto this by now. We don't fear the act of failing. We fear feeling the feelings associated with failing. Think back to a time you felt you failed, or someone told you failed, and relive that experience. What emotions come up for you? I think back to a time when an issue occurred with a student right at the end of the school day. It was brought to my attention after dismissal and I said I would investigate the situation first thing in the morning. After all students had been picked up for the day, I locked up the office and stayed late to catch up on some work. Meanwhile, a student who'd been involved with the reported incident shared what happened with the other student's parents. One of the parents came back to the school to talk with me. They were pounding on the front office door, hoping I was available. It was after hours and I was alone. I wasn't comfortable meeting with the parent with no one else around and I did not have any information to share, so I did not think meeting would be productive. I had the thought "There's nothing to talk about until tomorrow. It can wait." I avoided the conversation. I did not think it was a big deal.

Until it was.

The parent went to the superintendent the next morning and threatened to go to the local newspaper, saying they would do everything in their power to get me fired. The next morning, I was called to my superintendent's office. Fortunately, he was an amazingly supportive boss and we talked through it and created a plan of action. I later met with the parent and apologized for not meeting with them immediately. To me, this incident was an epic failure. I believe I failed in providing the best customer service possible and every time I think about that incident, I cringe with embarrassment and disappointment. Fortunately I was able to build a wonderful relationship with this family, but in that moment, I failed the parents and myself. My standard of success as a principal was to provide the best experience possible for every person that set foot on campus. I had failed my own expectations.

The feelings of disappointment, embarrassment, guilt, and shame that are associated with failure are among the most uncomfortable feelings we encounter. These agonizing emotions are the result of some agonizing thought patterns. When we think about failing at something, what do we make it mean? We usually make it mean that we are not good enough to achieve our goals, we are not capable enough to be successful, or that we don't have what it takes to make it. We start to compare ourselves to others around us, believing that they can be successful and we cannot. This leads us down the road to despair. We start creating thoughts from a place of scarcity and lack rather than from capability and abundance. When we believe we are not enough and personally do not have what it takes to be successful, we fail to try or we fail to continue.

You Cannot Fail – You Can Only Quit

This leads me to an important point regarding failure. If you are fully committed to accomplishing a goal, no matter what, then you will eventually achieve the goal. How is that possible? It is possible because you continue to take action until you reach the goal.

I call this taking massive action. When you have something you want to achieve and you are committed to it, no matter what obstacles get in your way or what fears come up, you must continue taking action until you reach the goal. You will have to analyze your approach from time to time and make adjustments along the way, but if you stay committed and focused on achieving what you really want, you can have anything.

I used to believe that failure was an absolute. You either succeeded or failed. Now that I've chosen not to make failure mean that I am inadequate, failure to me means learning. Every time you try an approach and it does not give you the results you wanted, you've learned what not to do. If you keep trying approaches until you reach the goal, all of the mini-failures along the way were intended to get you to the finish line. If you try an approach and it doesn't give you the results you want and you quit, only then have you truly failed. Failing only occurs when you quit because you've decided you have failed. Failing is learning. Quitting is failing.

This knowledge is so powerful because we can decide prior to taking action how we want to define our success and when we will call something a failure. Let's say you've done your internal thought work and you've decided that you are going to make a change in your career path. You feel passionate about education but you are not interested in being an administrator for the rest of your life. You've researched other career paths in education and learned that there is a demand for instructional consultants that provide trainings for school districts all over the country. Your love of travel and your passion for education combined into one sounds like a dream come true. The only problem is that the salary is about half of what you are earning now and it doesn't provide medical benefits. You do not see how you could afford to take such a hefty cut in pay. You feel trapped between having a job you love and earning a high wage. What if you aren't good at consulting and wind up hating the job? How do you decide whether you are going to go for it or continue working in a job you know is stable and comfortable?

When you feel the fear of failure creeping into a decision you are making, it's time to challenge the thoughts that are coming up. Here are some questions you can ask yourself to combat the fear of failure:

- What is it that I want to achieve?
- Why does achieving this matter?
- Am I willing to commit to achieving this goal no matter what?
- What will I do when I feel fear or frustration?
- How will I handle confusion and overwhelm?
- How will I handle obstacles that get in my way?
- Do I have a time limit to complete this achievement? If so, why?

- If I miss the time deadline, will I quit on my goal?
- What's the worst-case scenario if I achieve this goal?
- What's the worst-case scenario if I do not achieve this goal?

These questions are designed to shift your brain from focusing on all the ways you can fail to all the ways you have planned to protect yourself from failure. They will help you resolve your commitment to your decision and bolster your courage by acknowledging ahead of time that negative emotions will emerge and you have an action plan to combat the fear of failure.

Is It Ever OK to Quit?

I get this question a lot after I tell clients my theory that failing is learning and quitting is failing. They want to know if they are allowed to quit doing anything. My answer is always this: You are allowed to do anything you want! I am not a coach so that I can place judgment on people's decisions or tell you how to live. I coach to help you observe your thinking and intentionally choose whether you want to believe the thoughts you are having or not. You can always choose to stop taking action toward a goal. The key is to explore why you are considering quitting and decide from a place of empowerment.

I recently decided to sell my home. We lived there for 18 years and made so many memories during those years. My son was three months old when we moved in and we put it on the market just weeks after his high school graduation. I raised him as a single mom in this house and owning and maintaining this home was a badge of honor to me. I felt like selling it was a form of quitting that chapter of my life. I was torn between creating the lifestyle I'd been dreaming of for years and letting go of all I'd worked for in my past.

Through conversations with my coach and my husband, I was able to see that letting go of our home in order to pursue a location-independent lifestyle was part of the massive action we needed to take to achieve our macro goal of freedom to travel and work from anywhere in the world.

There is a difference between giving up and quitting and intentionally choosing to end or let go of something that no longer serves your greater mission. Giving up is when you still desire your goal, but you don't believe you will achieve it or you dislike the discomfort of the actions you need to take, so you stop taking action for immediate relief. It's wanting to take your dream vacation, but never booking it because you believe you'll never have the money or the time away from work to go. You don't research travel options and discounts, put any money away in a travel savings account, or ask for the time off because you don't want to save money or ask your boss for the time off. You still strongly desire to go, but you are giving up on taking the trip because you do not believe it's possible and you don't want to feel the discomfort that comes from doing the things required to take the trip. This is quitting on yourself and your dreams.

When you intentionally choose to end taking action toward something, it is either because you have achieved what you wanted to achieve or you have decided that the act of stopping action toward something in order to fulfill a different desire is necessary. As in the case with my home, in order for me to fulfill my dream of building a business to support educators that was location-independent, I had to let go of my past accomplishments. This meant quitting my job and quitting paying a substantial mortgage. Choosing to quit doing these two things was not painful once I realized they were simply part of the action plan required to achieve my goal. While it is not emotionally easy to intentionally quit, it is a part of the process for evolving your life and experiencing everything you want to experience in this lifetime. So, my lovely, the answer to whether you should quit or not comes down to this: What are you giving up by quitting?

Summary

- Decide to commit no matter what.
- Define success and failure ahead of time.
- Take massive action.
- Be willing to adjust your approach until you reach your goal.
- When you want to quit, ask yourself why and choose intentionally.
- Failure is Learning.
- Quitting is Failure.

11

Living an Emotionally Fit Life

B y now, you are gaining awareness of your thoughts and you may be starting to question some of them, yet your brain is wondering how to process all of this information and turn it into a way of being. I'll share some of my routines that will help you get started with creating a lifestyle of emotional fitness.

Ways to Change your Emotional Vibe

1. Start and End with Gratitude

Gratitude and resistance cannot coexist. Start and end the day listing all the things available to you that you feel grateful for. In the morning, begin with a focus on gratitude for your well-being, then let your gratitude spiral out to other people you love. Feel grateful for the upcoming day and all the opportunities that day is going to provide. In the evening, focus your gratitude on what went well that day. Sink deep into the vibrations of gratefulness. You can even choose to feel gratitude for the things that did not go well by viewing them as lessons. What did you learn from those bumps in the road and how might you adjust your approach?

2. Change Your Emotional Energy Level

One of the fastest ways to change your emotional state is to change your physical state. When you are feeling low levels of emotional energy, get your body moving. Take a walk, stretch, lift your arms above your head, do jumping jacks – anything that gets your blood flowing. If you are at work and not able to get up and move around, you can also create energy by quick, deep inhales through your nose. I find that increasing my oxygen intake does wonders for stifled thinking. When I need more energy, I take short, quick breaths. When I am emotionally charged and want to calm my energy, I take deep, slow breaths. Your body and your mind are interrelated, so a shift in your physical energy will impact your mental and emotional energy.

3. Rest / Work / Play / Repeat

All human beings need rest, work, and play in their lives. We ensure children have a balance of these three activities, but as adults we tend to focus on our work and slight our need for rest and play. I am certainly guilty of this! One way to check your R-W-P balance is to write down all of the activities you participate in on a weekly basis, including your evenings and weekends, then sort each activity into one of the three categories. Notice whether you have a more proportioned approach or a heavy imbalance between activities. If you are lacking in one of the areas, challenge yourself to dedicate some more time to it and see if your emotional vibe shifts. The three areas do not need to be precisely even, but you will find that when your rest and play needs have been met, work gets so much more enjoyable.

4. Treat Yourself Like a Child

Oftentimes when our emotional energy is low, we add insult to injury by being unkind to ourselves. We say things like, "I'm so stupid. Why can't I figure this out? I'll never get this. I hate the way I handled that." Negative self-talk is natural, but never necessary. It is a window into our level of self-esteem and it produces valuable information about how we view ourselves and the world around us.

The way you talk to yourself is the example you are setting for others. When you find that you are talking negatively to yourself, write down all the things you say to yourself. Read them back and listen to how terrible they sound. Then, read them again and imagine you are saying them to your own child or a student you adore. You will find that you are horrified at the thought of saying these things to a child, yet you are fine with saying them to yourself. Choose one that is most upsetting to you and run a STEAR cycle on it. See if you can find an alternate thought to consider and a kinder way to speak to yourself. The kinder you can be with yourself, the more open you will find yourself to trying new things and taking leaps of faith.

Beware of Internal Wars

When you learn to self-coach, there will be times of clarity and times of cloudiness. You may cognitively understand that you have a thought that is blocking a result you want, but be unable to change your approach. This usually indicates that you have opposing belief systems looping in your brain.

What this means is that you believe two opposing thoughts. For example, you may believe the thought "I really need this job." You also may fully believe the thought "I am ready for a career change." Your brain bounces back and forth between these opposing beliefs and finds itself short-circuiting. This is often when we say we feel confused. When you find yourself in confusion, see if you can identify two thoughts that oppose one another. Run a STEAR cycle on each of them separately to see what emotion and approach each thought creates. Then drop into your heart and compare the two. Is there a thought that more resonates with you? Does one feel better than the other? If so, allow that thought to determine your approach. That is your essential self speaking. The other thought is coming from your social self. It is basically your brain and your soul having a discussion and it is up to you to decide which side you will allow to lead.

Personal Goal Planning

A healthy part of living an emotionally fit life is goal planning. If you are anything like me, you feel nauseated at the thought of setting goals. Goal setting, at least the way I've experienced it in the past, was arduous because I made it mean I was setting myself up for failure, negative feedback, and feelings of shame and guilt. When I believed that these were going to be my outcomes, I subconsciously set the goals at a lower level so I was guaranteed to meet them. Ironically, when you set the bar low, you are kidding no one, especially not yourself. What happens when you set the bar low for yourself is that you feel no sense of accomplishment when you meet or surpass the goal. Your brain already knows it is capable of that goal, so it does not generate feelings of excitement and pride.

Setting the bar low can actually have a negative effect. Since your brain believes that it will require little effort to achieve the goal, you may find yourself not giving much energy and attention to ensuring goal completion, which can sabotage your achievement of that goal.

But what about massive, or macro, goals? Should you set a goal so big that your brain does not even comprehend how to start? My answer is a resounding yes. Here's why: I believe that anything you desire in life is possible to have or you would not have the capacity to desire it. If you truly believed it was not possible, your brain would not generate thoughts around it. Perhaps you have a secret desire to write a book, or travel to Spain, or learn how to sail. You would not desire these things if it were not possible for you to achieve them. The issue arises when we have a desire we do not think is obtainable. We have the desire, "I want to own a private jet," and our brain immediately tells us there's no way we can accomplish this. The brain thinks this thought because it wants to focus on the how. It wants to know how we will go from being a school principal to an entrepreneur who owns her own plane. The gap is so wide that the brain cannot imagine the steps one needs to take in order to get from A to B. Your brain also kicks into protection mode by telling you not to consider pursuing such macro goals because you will feel disappointed if you don't achieve it. This is why we back down from writing macro goals.

Macro Goals

On the flip side, the reason you should write macro goals is that they are exhilarating to dream. They raise your emotional vibration to its highest state. It is from this place that you can start to develop your approach. Think of something so wild that you can barely imagine it coming true, something that if it actually happened, you would be pinching yourself to see if it were real. Go through this experience in your mind as if you were physically present. Notice the heightened vibrations in your body. Feel the thrill of the experience, the rush of accomplishment, and the pride of your efforts.

This person, who is in the moment of success, is the person you must become if you want to fulfill your wildest dreams. Who is she? How does she live? What are her daily routines? Who does she spend her time with? What does she love to do with her day? What is her energy level? How does she interact with people? What does she contribute to the world? Take time to explore life from this heightened emotional state.

Micro Goals

When you step into the emotional energy of a person who's already achieved your macro goal, you will be able to devise a set of micro goals that put your macro goal within view. Let's say you want to tour Europe for the summer and you envision yourself walking through the streets of Rome, Paris, Munich, and Vienna. You can see the sights in your mind and smell the street vendors. You can feel the cobblestone streets under your feet and the gratitude in your heart that you are in Europe. When you imagine this, your body responds as though it has already happened. From this emotional energy, you ask yourself the following questions:

- How did you make this happen?
- What small steps did I take to get here?
- If I did know how to accomplish this goal, what would I do?
- What is one small thing I can start today to get me closer to my goal?
- What did I have to commit to in order to achieve my dream?

The tips and strategies you receive from your highest self will transform your dreams from hopeful wishes to tangible realities.

Micro Fails

In the midst of the emotional fitness journey, there will be results you deem as failures. You'll miss a meeting, forget to return a call, make a financial investment that doesn't provide a return, say something you regret, or fail to submit your work on time. Part of self-coaching is the ability to take a look at these situations and put them in perspective. When you are boldly living the life you were meant to live, you will inevitably take some risks. These risks will usually be intentional and as calculated as possible; however, you will still be faced with unexpected results from time to time.

The key to recovering from miscalculations is to assess the situation. Ask yourself what worked, what did not work, and how you can adjust your approach toward achieving your macro goal. Notice what parts of your assessment are facts and what aspects are your opinion of what happened. Allow yourself to feel the disappointment of the undesired result.

I find it helpful to give myself a set amount of time to feel the disappointment. This helps me not slip into despair or blame. I give myself five minutes to feel badly about my mistake, then I ask, "Now what?" Review your macro goals and determine how this approach was misaligned and how you might adjust and keep on going. Remind yourself that failure is learning and quitting is failing. Reconnect with your compelling reasons for achieving your macro goals and recommit to doing whatever it takes, including micro fails, in order to make those dreams reality.

Macro Wins

Micro fails seem to diminish when you keep your focus on the big wins. I realize that none of us want to feel the disappointment of a failed attempt. However, being willing to feel disappointment in the short term is the secret sauce for long-term wins. As financial coach Dave Ramsey says, "If you can live like no one else, then later you can live like no one else." I interpret this as the willingness to endure some negative emotion in your journey in order to embrace the positive emotion that comes with achieving massive goals. Our need for immediate gratification and comfort at all times slows or halts our progress toward macro goals. Keep your focus on the big picture, what you really want, why you really want it, and your resiliency for feeling the disappointment of micro fails will build.

My Wish for You

Here is the best secret in this book. Are you ready for it? This one revelation changed the way I experienced every day of my life. Here it is: You cannot make a wrong decision! You can live an empowered life regardless of which path you choose.

You bought this book because you feel torn between learning to love the job you are in versus wanting so badly to leave. You want to love the job because that would make life so much easier. You would not have to come up with an alternate plan, take the courageous step of leaving, or worry about upsetting others. You want to make yourself enjoy the position as school leader, yet you continue to feel overwhelm, exhaustion, and disdain. You are starting to think that no amount of money is worth feeling this badly, but the thought of stepping away scares you to death. It feels like your future is hanging on this one decision: Love the job or leave it?

Imagine if you did not have to make a decision about your job. Assume there is no decision to be made, no pressure to make the right decision, and no way for you to make a wrong decision. How would you approach your day? What if staying was the right choice and leaving was the right choice? What would you do then?

When you believe that you cannot make a wrong decision, you drop the resistance and fear that comes with believing there is a right and wrong decision. You start to see the blessings that are available to you in your current position and you start to explore the possibilities of other experiences. You create your life's work from a place of knowing there is no wrong way, there are no incorrect choices, and every decision you make is the right one at that time. You always have the option to adjust your approach. You always have the option to change your mind.

With the tools in this book, you have the ability to manage your thoughts and emotions to the point of truly loving your principalship. You can work through thoughts that bring you stress and seek alternate thoughts that bring you more joy and peace. You can work toward loving the job and being fully present and engaged in the work you do. Deciding to enjoy yourself in your current position is always available to you.

You can also, from an empowered state, choose to lovingly leave the position. You can move forward with new experiences and be grateful for the knowledge that you have gained during your tenure.

You can also have the desire to leave your job yet stay for the immediate future. Your desire can fuel your dedication to making a massive action plan as you continue to work until you are ready to leave. You can coach yourself through the process of being in a job that is not your ideal working conditions while you are taking steps toward your exit plan.

There is no wrong path. Whichever decision you make is the right decision for you until it isn't. When it no longer becomes the decision you want, adjust your approach and make a new decision.

My ultimate wish for you is that you are able to generate thoughts that bring you joy regardless of your job or any other situation you find yourself experiencing. You have the ability to feel empowered from within at any time. No job can take that away from you. No boss or other person can take away your personal power. You can choose to show up at your current job and be the best darn principal there ever was because you consciously are choosing to be the best version of yourself every single day. You can choose to resign from your job with a level of courage and commitment, knowing that you have what it takes to succeed in following your deepest passion. Simply knowing you have the power over your life can change the way you show up for the rest of your life.

Summary

- Gratitude and resistance cannot coexist.
- Your physical fitness is directly connected to your emotional fitness.

- Personal goal planning is fun when it is driven by your essential self.
- Focus on macro goals, not micro fails.
- There is no such thing as a wrong decision.

12

The Empowered Principal

Congratulations! You are to be celebrated! You have chosen to enter into emotional adulthood where you take ownership and responsibility for your own emotions. This is an accomplishment that few people deliberately pursue. The work is simple, yet challenging. It requires extreme patience, practice, and humility on our part. Learning to question your thoughts, feel your emotions, and consciously choose your approach to situations is the most empowered way of being I know. I commend you for your commitment and courage.

The Rebirth of You

When you actively engage in emotional fitness training, you evolve into a new version of yourself. You will feel different internally and you may experience an urge to change your external appearance. The way you view yourself and the world around you will shift. Whether you stay in your current position or you decide to leave, you will be a new you.

This may feel alarming at first. You'll notice that you respond differently than you once did. You'll note that things have a different meaning to you and that thoughts you were once extremely attached to no longer carry so much weight. There is a lightness that comes with emotional fitness, which may feel strange at times, as if you aren't worrying enough or caring enough. Just know that all of this is a natural part of the process. You are building a new relationship with yourself and with those around you. It's like meeting someone new for the first time. You'll want to be kind, patient, and respectful with yourself. Your new self may feel strange at times, but it is a strangeness that feels exciting and loving. Embrace this new you and prepare to experience what it is like to live from an internally empowered state.

Change Back Attacks

Martha Beck explains that when our internal transformations become apparent to other people, they may be uncomfortable and want you to change back to the old you. They will do and say things with the hope that you will revert back to your former way of being. At times, their attempts to keep themselves comfortable can be harsh and hurtful.

Understand that their actions are about the way *they* are feeling. It has nothing to do with you. It can be painful to have others reject the new version of you and attempt to manipulate you into going back to the status quo, but you can handle it by listening with your full attention, acknowledging their frustration, staying true to yourself, and offering love and support.

You Will Still Have Bad Days

Emotional fitness is not a cure for bad days or negative emotions. You will still experience days where things do not go smoothly, obstacles arise, and you are unhappy. As my master coach, Brooke, reminds us, "We are going to feel negative emotion about 50 percent of our life. It's a part of the human experience." Our goal is not to avoid all negative emotion; it is to be able and willing to experience *all* emotions. It is knowing that no matter what emotions are triggered, we are capable of feeling them, they cannot physically hurt us, and they will pass.

We want to run interference when our brain tells us that we are going to die if we allow negative emotions to be present. So often we believe that we want to avoid feeling badly at all costs. This could not be further from the truth. Our strength lies in our ability to feel any emotion, positive or negative. The difference between resisting bad days and allowing them to come and go lies within you.

Resisting our bad days comes from a mental state of external blame. We think that the situations occurring throughout the day are the reason we are having a bad day, so we complain, dramatize, and buffer. Allowing our bad days means living from a mental state of acceptance and responsibility. We understand that the situation is not the problem; our thoughts about it are creating our emotional response. When we can remind ourselves of this, we can redirect our thinking to more proactive thoughts.

Then there will just be some days where you are not able to manage your thoughts in real time as events occur.

It is going to happen. It's ok. When you find yourself in the middle of a bad day, treat yourself the way you would treat your best friend. Say comforting things to yourself. Listen. Acknowledge. Remind her that tomorrow will be a better day, no matter what they say.

This Work Is Forever

Know that emotional fitness is exactly like physical fitness. When you first begin, it will feel cumbersome. You'll have limited stamina and be tempted to quit. You'll have setbacks. When you slack off, you'll notice. You have to keep practicing and participating for the remainder of your life. If you keep trying and adjusting along the way, you'll wake up one day and notice you can run a little longer, lift a little more weight, and breathe a little more freely. The work is not glamorous, but it is extremely rewarding. Be prepared to commit to your emotional well-being for life.

I often ask my coach why I am still working on the same unintentional thoughts over and over again. I want to fix it once and for all! She has to remind me that thought work is like breathing. We're rarely aware that is happening in the background all day long to keep us alive. When something suppresses our breath and we struggle to inhale, our breath quickly comes into our full awareness and we must attend to it in order to continue surviving.

The same is true with our thoughts. Thoughts occur in the brain all day long and we do not pay attention to most of them. Our emotions are the attention signal that brings us back to thought awareness. You can only question a thought once it is in your awareness. As you gain emotional durability, you'll uncover thoughts new to your awareness. Accept thought work in your life as you accept breathing. It feels so much better to allow than to resist and hold your breath.

Last, but Not Least

You initially purchased this book because you were miserable in your career as a school leader. You believed this position would hold such promise and potential and that you would finally have some authority to instill positive change. Instead, you found yourself dazed and confused, feeling like there was no hope for change. You have been teetering between wanting to enjoy your job and wanting to leave the profession. You now know that: 1) you cannot make a wrong decision, 2) there are no mistakes, 3) you have the power within you to feel better about the work you do, or 4) you can courageously decide to leave the profession with the knowing that you will be successful in your new endeavors.

If You Decide to Stay

The strategies in this book may have been the missing link for you. If you have been applying this information in your daily life, you may be in the process of shifting to thoughts that trigger more positive emotions about your job.

This is fantastic news! You have realized that your calling is the field of education and you now feel more aligned to the work you've chosen. I must say I am so impressed with your decision and the work you've done to turn your thinking around. I have been in your shoes and know the work is not easy. Continue self-coaching on every situation that brings up intense emotional reactions. If you ever get stuck and need further support, let's connect so I can walk you through it, one step at a time.

If You Decide to Go

If, on the other hand, you've read this book and it has inspired you to create an action plan for a career change, congratulations! You have done the work to recognize your true calling and to steer closer toward a life that feels good to you. This is courageous and empowered living!

Know that if you aren't able to immediately depart, you have the tools you need to manage your thinking while you are preparing your exit plan. Keep in mind that you must make the decision to leave from a place of authentic integrity and alignment with your essential self. Believing that changing your situation (quitting this job for another one) will make you feel better is living under the presumption that outside circumstances control our emotions. I can tell you from personal experience that this is not true. The way you do anything is the way you do everything. If you quit your job only because you want out in order to feel better, then you will find that your thinking and emotions come with you, regardless of what work you choose to do. You must first learn to become aware of your thoughts, question their validity, and manage your emotions and approach to life. Otherwise, leaving this job for another serves no useful purpose.

If you can learn to manage your mind in your most stressful of circumstances, then you can certainly manage your mind when it comes to the work you feel passionate about. Depending on your choice in careers, you may find yourself working longer and harder than ever.

I consciously chose to resign from my school leadership position in order to build a business that supports school leaders. It was my true passion and calling. I resisted the call for years, but those years in school leadership gifted me with the experience needed to develop my coaching business. I spent seven years learning from coaches how to manage my mind while still working as a principal. I slowly developed an action plan while continuing to work until I knew it was time. When my mom fell ill and the structure of the school year no longer served me, I knew it was a sign that it was my time to transition into my coaching practice full-time. And here is what happened – when I finally left the job I was so anxious to be away from, I found myself faced with new challenges and negative emotions.

Building a business from scratch brings an entirely new set of frustrations and waves of overwhelm and confusion. Thought work does not cease to exist from a change in career or job location. It will only cease to exist when your mind no longer produces thoughts. The fundamental difference between managing my mind in my education career and managing my mind now is that I love the work I do. I liked education; I love coaching. I am willing to feel tired, overworked, frustrated, confused, overwhelmed, and inexperienced.

I want this for you my friend. I want you to want to be willing to experience negative emotion. This difference is everything.

Do the work.

Be empowered.

Make intentional decisions.

I am here to help when you are ready.

Sending love and strength, Angela

Recommended Reads

Daring Greatly by Brené Brown
Finding Your Own North Star by Martha Beck
Loving What Is by Byron Katie
Self Coaching 101 by Brooke Castillo
The Element by Sir Ken Robinson
Unleash the Power Within by Anthony Robbins

Acknowledgments

This book has been a long time in the making. I've known since I was a little girl that I someday would become an author. I always wanted to be more verbally articulate, yet the words always seemed to flow best through my hands. I thank my Grampie Kelly for this. He was a poet and I am sure he gifted his talent to me when he left this earth years ago. This book is a physical manifestation of my love and gratitude for him.

Writing for joy is one thing. I enjoy writing in my journal, writing weekly newsletters for my tribe, writing letters to family and friends, and even writing reference letters for former employees! However, committing to completing a book from cover to cover is a level up from the day-to-day writing I am used to. Just like buying a house or having your first child, there is never "the right time" to write a book. And that was the case for me. I'd first met Angela Lauria through The Life Coach School. She presented at one of Brooke Castillo's annual mastermind seminars. I was enamored with her story and her work. I wanted to write a book but I did not know anything about the publishing industry or the details of what completing a book entailed. I followed Angela on Facebook for two years before I decided to pull the trigger and apply to her program. In my mind, I could hear my social self-saying this wasn't exactly the right time to be taking on one more thing. Yet my essential self was screaming, "Yes! This is *exactly* the right time for this book to be born. Let's do it!"

I listened to her this time and went all in, making it through the interview process and into the Author Incubator program. I learned that Angela and I were not only connected through The Life Coach School, we both studied life coaching under Martha Beck! My essential self-confirmed that I was following my North Star and on my destiny's path.

Speaking of my path, I cannot express enough gratitude for Martha and Brooke. Their work literally changed the entire course of my life. Until I met them and studied their teachings, I had no idea that I had any amount of control over my thoughts, emotions, and my life. It was through them that I met Angela and was able to bring this book to fruition. Thank you, amazing women, for your work in the world and for showing up so courageously and authentically. You all are the example of what is possible.

To the Morgan James Publishing team: Special thanks to David Hancock, CEO & Founder for believing in me and my message. To my Author Relations Manager, Gayle West, thanks for making the process seamless and easy. Many more thanks to everyone else, but especially Jim Howard, Bethany Marshall, and Nickcole Watkins.

To my former school district, I am so appreciative of the endless opportunities I've been given as member of the team. Not only did I gain tremendous experience and knowledge while working with you, I developed the deepest and dearest friendships with my colleagues. I would love to name you all here, but given my 22 years in the district, that would require an entirely separate book! I will shout out to one special person – Cathy – who has earned my love and respect for eternity. You are truly a diamond in the rough.

To my business coach and dear friend, Stacey Smith, there are not words to thank you for how you've impacted my life. You welcomed me, loved me, coached me, and believed in me. Meeting you has been one of the greatest gifts of my life. Thank you for showing up 100% as you, for being willing to be vulnerable and honest, and for taking me in as a fellow coach. Your compassion and empathy will forever be etched on my heart.

To my tribe, thank you for taking time to follow my work, watch my Facebook live videos, and spread my message with like-minded folks. It is an honor to serve you in the largest capacity I can and I appreciate the opportunity to support clients with massive breakthroughs. I genuinely love helping other people see their own power. It is a joy that has no words to describe it. It fills my heart over brim to hear stories of emotional transformation. Carry on, brave souls. You were meant for this work. Together we can bring emotional well-being to schools, teachers, parents, and our youth.

To my family, I thank you for allowing me to be myself. I know I am not an easy person to have in the family, but I do love you all and my work is a testament to how I was raised. My grandma is my sweetest fan – she always comes in with a smile, a great story, and amazing desserts. My mom is my biggest fan – always has been and always will be. She watches every video, reads every post, and is sure to put in her two cents! I love her for that so much. My dad is my proudest fan – seeing him beam with pride over my accomplishments and having him text me his funny thoughts of the day is everything to me. My one and only sister, Miss Heather Kelly, is my most supportive fan – calling me daily to congratulate me, give feedback and support, check in on my mental well-being, and to love on me when no one else did. Thank you for understanding when I wasn't able to pick up and for being relentless in your commitment to our friendship and to my mission. You are a true rock star.

To my inner circle, Susan, Kathy, Karen, Andrea, and Anita – or as I lovingly refer to them, The Old Guard – my gratefulness for our 20+ years of friendship as kindergarten colleagues and girls weekend partners has no bounds. We were a powerhouse team back in the day and we are a powerhouse team today. We are a team for life! So much love for you all.

To my website designer, my parenting compadre, close friend, and lifesaver, I thank Kathryn Holland Besser for her boundless support and love not just for me, but for my son and family. I strive to emulate her love and compassion for others.

To Emily and Jessica, my hookers (inside joke), thank you for standing by my side through all the drama. I am so lucky to have friends like you. You exude the meaning of friendship and loyalty. Donde sea que vivamos, siempre estaremos conectados. Además, siempre habrá chismes! LOL

Finally, to my son Alex and my love Mitch. Thank you for your patience – Lord knows you need it living with me! Thank you for your unconditional love. Thank you for your sense of humor, your gentleness, and acceptance. You two are my everything and I live my life to honor you both. May my legacy make you proud.

About the Author

Angela Kelly Robeck is well versed in teaching and school leadership, having been a teacher for over 15 years and a school principal for six years prior to moving into a district level position. She is a certified life coach of The Life Coach School and completed the life coaching program from Martha Beck International, and founded Angela Kelly Coaching. She specializes in helping school leaders employ their empowerment and build emotional resiliency.

During her tenure as principal, Angela was disillusioned and in a constant state of frustration over the lack of control she felt in her position. After years of searching for support and solutions, she boldly chose to leave her district of 22 years and devote herself to creating support for school leaders. Combining her years of expertise in education with her passion of personal development, Angela offers individual and group coaching programs that transform the careers of educators.

Angela deeply understands the emotional toll of educational leadership and how it profoundly impacts people's lives. She works with site and district leaders to help them create more satisfying lives both professionally and personally.

Angela recently moved to the beaches of Santa Cruz, CA, from Silicon Valley. She lives with her husband, Mitchell and they have one son, Alex, who is currently studying screenwriting at Chapman University. She loves spending time with her friends and family, traveling, listening to music, wine-tasting, and walks along the beach.

Thank You

My empowered principal, I hope this book has brought new insights to you, both personally and professionally. It was my complete honor to write this book just for you. I sincerely thank you for taking time to read this and for courageously being a role model of what is possible as a school leader. I would love to spread this wealth of knowledge to all school leaders across the country, as I believe this work is where we begin true educational reform. Not only for students, but for the adults who devote their careers to educating our nation's children. I am relentlessly committed to bringing emotional fitness to all those in education as I firmly believe it is the missing link in our schools today. I ask that if you found this book helpful, you share it with your fellow colleagues. Having others around you understand these concepts will further strengthen your emotional resilience as you can hold high-level conversations where all parties are taking ownership of their thoughts and emotional responses.

Anytime I read a book that has moved me, I have initial momentum to integrate changes into my life, which eventually wanes and I slip back into my previous routines and lifestyle. It's natural, especially when you are doing it alone. I've done this a hundred times! Fortunately, this is not the end of your support. I have additional resources to help you along the way. Depending on how deep you want to dive into this work and how quickly you want transformation, you can choose the following options:

a. Use this book as a reference at any time.

b. Follow me on Facebook, Instagram, Twitter, and Linked In: @akellycoaching #theempoweredprincipalpodcast

c. Sign up for The Empow WORD weekly email. Don't worry. It's short, sweet, and free. I hate reading long emails, so I won't take up much of your inbox. www.angelakellycoaching.com/downloads

d. Listen to The Empowered Principal Podcast. You can find me on iTunes, Stitcher, Spotify, or any other podcast app out there! It's also always free.

e. Download my Free Quick Start Guide which aligns to the first three podcast episodes at: www.angelakellycoaching.com/downloads

f. Apply to work with me directly. Visit: https://angelakellycoachingschedule.as.me/ to set up a complementary, no obligation, 30-minute discovery call to see how we can create further transformation for you. This call is such a fun way for us to meet and explore a personalized coaching relationship. I love connecting with my like-minded souls and cannot wait to meet you!